HOLIDAY HANDBOOK

Wrap Up a Carefree Christmas!

By Jacquelyne Kramer Koche

HOUR   PRESS

San Rafael

California

Published by:

HOUR   PRESS
P.O. Box 12743, Northgate Station
San Rafael, CA 94913-2743

Typography by QuadraType, San Francisco
Printing and Binding: Braun-Brumfield, Inc., Ann Arbor, Michigan

First Printing April 1987
Second Printing (revised edition) September 1987
Printed in the United States of America

Library of Congress Cataloging in Publication Data.

Koche, Jacquelyne Kramer
  Holiday Handbook
  Wrap Up a Carefree Christmas!

1. Christmas
2. Shopping—Directories
3. Christmas—Psychological aspects.
I. Title
GT4985.K57   1987   394.2′68282   86-21389
ISBN   0-939131-00-5

To George, who makes it Christmas every day of the year, and to my children, Kerry, Kevin, Kamelle and Kristen, who decorate our family tree with their beauty.

With appreciation to everyone at the Sonoma Index-Tribune, with whom I worked so many happy years, and especially to Robert Lynch, Editor and Publisher, and John Lynch, Managing Editor, who allowed me to grow with their award-winning newspaper.

ABOUT THE AUTHOR:

Jacquelyne Kramer Koche has won twelve national and state journalism awards, and her articles have been featured in many magazines with national circulation. She is a member of California Writers Club and Sigma Delta Chi (Society of Professional Journalists).

The former newspaper feature writer, who holds a Master's degree in Counseling, has done crisis intervention work as well as family counseling. She understands well the crises that the holiday season poses for many.

Through interviews and research into what it takes to make Christmas the joyous occasion it should be, this mother of four has put together a wise and often witty book on coping with the holidays.

What others are saying:

"Perhaps the most comprehensive guide available today on coping with every aspect of the Christmas season."

(Ideas for Better Living)

"Few books offer such innovative gift-giving ideas combining budget considerations with effective organization and time management."

(Midwest Book Review)

"Commended as excellent. Good writing, well-presented, profoundly interesting. Justly earned words of praise for work this outstanding."

(WYOU-TV)

"Destined to be this season's best seller."

(Volunteers in Action newsletter)

"A fantastic book! Takes the crowded shopping centers, aching feet, not enough time and even less money, headaches and stress out of Christmas." *(Book Dealers World)*

"A quality package. Well-organized, well-researched text that covers all aspects of preparing for the holidays." *(Sonoma Index-Tribune)*

"Buy this brimful-of-great-ideas book and make the dream of a carefree holiday season come true. Humor, wisdom, understanding and love. . .a book that combines everything." *(MSPA journal)*

DISCLAIMER

TABLE OF CONTENTS

CHRISTMAS LAMENT

It's two weeks till Christmas,
Your budgets awry.
Not a creature is helping,
Your strength has run dry.

No gifts lie hidden
In closets' deep gloom;
Your list of tasks undone
Could fill a room.

What you need is some aid,
A way out of duress,
A book that shows how
To relieve your distress.

What to do first
And what to do not at all,
Will lead to a Christmas
Remembered next Fall.

Turn the pages, dear reader,
Heed their advice on the way
And Christmas this year
Will be a memorable day!

Introduction

Congratulations!

You have decided to do something constructive about preparing for the holidays. You are not going to be intimidated anymore by the flurry of activity that begins in November and doesn't end until January 2 the following year.

Your "Holiday Handbook" will:

1. Provide you with a Christmas Card Record that will take you to the year 2001.

2. List over 150 firms specializing in mail order, with a comprehensive guide to shopping by mail.

3. Help you create a year-around gift buying plan that will keep the holidays financially feasible.

4. Give you tips on selecting creative gifts for those on your Christmas list.

5. Show you how to trim your Christmas card list, deal with card-sending in alternative ways, or even eliminate it.

6. Provide Gift Profile record sheets for important people in your life.

7. Present gift ideas that are low cost and can be sent by mail.

8. Show you great ideas for the last-minute shopper, as well as interesting stocking stuffers and hostess gifts.

9. Help you plan your holiday party.

10. Give you a comprehensive guide to gift wrapping and mailing.

You Can Make Christmas a Beautiful Event

As "Holiday Handbook" unfolds, you will discover there is no one perfect way to cope with the Yuletide season—there is only YOUR way, and that is always the right way.

As you fill out the worksheets, you will find ways to create a Christmas that is personally yours—the Christmas you've always wanted, one that will leave you with a feeling of peace and contentment that will last into the new year.

Begin Now . . .
    . . . to discover the happiness Christmas can bring!

1.

Getting Organized

If the very mention of Christmas makes you think of crowded shopping centers, headaches, stress, aching feet, not enough time and even less money—you're not alone!

"Each year about the middle of December I start to panic," admits 32-year-old Lynne, who has a busy job in public relations and is also the mother of two sons under eight years of age.

"I know it sounds crazy, but I keep thinking if I just ignore it, maybe Christmas will go away. I'm never prepared, and it's gotten so I hate the holiday season. I don't like to feel this way, but I just can't help it."

Lynne ruefully admits that although she prepares holiday press releases far in advance of the Christmas season as part of her job, she somehow has never been able to coordinate her own holiday efforts.

With nearly 60 percent of American women now in the work force, most wives and mothers agree with Lynne that just keeping up with daily tasks is stressful enough. The thought of adding holiday planning to this daily burden, when Christmas is still far away, seems impossible.

However, with a little advance planning, that roller-coaster season that begins with Thanksgiving in November and ends with New Year's Day in January can finally be brought under control.

Picture yourself free to enjoy the beauty and true meaning of the season with family and friends, all because you were able to spare two or three hours each month for advance preparation.

Create the Plan that is Right for You

No single plan is correct for everyone. You must decide what feels right for you, and then personalize it so it truly reflects you and your situation.

Some people enjoy planning Christmas in every detail, while

3

others prefer a few surprises at the end even if this means doing some things at the last minute.

Some save money throughout the year especially for the holidays, while others like to charge gifts and pay for them later the following year.

However, one fact that holds true for everyone is the necessity for making some kind of plan for the holidays.

Holiday Planning Guide

Like Lynne, few adults have unmixed feelings about this event, which occasions such joyous anticipation in our children. However, there are ways to make the holidays happier for everyone. You will make it happen for you by following a few simple suggestions.

• Decide who's in charge. No battle was ever won without a general to create the plan. If you're the one who will be responsible for Christmas this year, don't waste time feeling sorry for yourself because you have to do it.

Instead, create a plan that will enlist the support of everyone from family and friends to spouse, roommate, sweetheart, or children.

• Make a list of everything you have to do. Keep a notebook in your handbag for ideas that occur to you at work, and a master calendar at home. You'll need lots of space, so don't settle for one of those miniature calendars that have room for only the date and a few brief words.

• This year, no matter what month you purchased this book, check the annual calendar on page 85 for tasks that must be done before Christmas. Transfer necessary items to your master calendar.

• An absolute "must"—Make sure you pencil in at least four hours each week free time for yourself. Even if you only stay at home and repair to the bathroom for a wonderful, steamy bubble bath and facial, this is relaxing time for you.

Without it, tension will continue to mount, which can set you back days if illness results. Remember, without you, the commanding general, there can be no task force!

• Each evening before bed, plan what pre-holiday tasks you will accomplish tomorrow. List them in order of importance, so if you're not able to finish every one, the most important ones will get done first.

• If you have children, begin now assigning them special jobs within their capabilities. Perhaps they can help organize your gift wrap box, finding scissors, cellophane tape, gift ribbon and paper, tags and seals.

They can make their own gift lists and plan a shopping budget. If they are old enough, they can help address and stamp family Christmas cards as well as their own. Younger children can create their own special art work for the holidays which can be used as gifts for relatives or artistic gift wrap paper.

• Planning to take your children on a shopping trip to help them buy gifts for those on their holiday list? Do consider taking each child on a separate day or evening, perhaps one evening after work on a night the stores are open late.

Combine a festive dinner out, and give the very special gift of your individual time to help your son or daughter shop for gifts for friends and family. Things will go more quickly this way, and it will be an evening to remember for both of you.

• Do not take children shopping, however, until they have an idea of price and gift possibilities for each person on their list. It is easier then, when confronted at a store with an expensive item your child may want to buy, to let her see that buying that gift might use all the budgeted money, with no funds left for gifts for others on her list.

Remember, planning in advance sets up good habit patterns for your child in other areas, also.

• Plan ahead so you can avoid some of the small Christmas crises you know are inevitable. For those nights when you've worked all day and spent the evening holiday shopping, try to have extra casseroles in the freezer to heat and eat, or consider patronizing the local pizza parlor.

• For those unexpected gifts you receive, do keep several generic gifts, already wrapped, on hand. (See Chapter Eight, Hostess Gift Ideas). Also, buy at least a dozen more Christmas cards than you feel you will need.

• Create "errand day" one afternoon each week. This way you can consolidate tasks you might otherwise have scattered during the week. This will create more free time.

That day you can carpool the children, pick up the cleaning, have a prescription refilled and do your grocery shopping. Plan a pre-cooked freezer dinner for that evening's meal.

• Keep a list of alternative baby sitters you can call on if your regular sitter is unavailable or ill and you have a "must attend" event on your calendar.

• Buy all the Christmas stamps you will need as soon as they go on sale at the post office. Keep stamps, cards and other holiday materials in a specific place in one room of the house so you won't spend precious minutes rounding up everything you need.

• Add your own tips here:

_____

_____

_____

_____

Basic Decisions You Must Make

The following Christmas quiz has been designed to help you in your holiday planning efforts. As you answer the questions, mark your appointment calendar with dates on which certain tasks must be done.

That way you can easily look ahead and see what needs to be done and not overload any one week.

Add suggestions to yourself in the Christmas notebook you are keeping, tasks that don't require being done on a special date but ones, nevertheless, that you don't want to forget.

By following the suggestions on these pages and answering the Christmas Quiz you will:

• Have more time to spend with family and friends.
• Create a workable holiday plan, designed just for YOU.
• Feel in control of, rather than controlled by the season.
• Design a budget to fit the holidays, instead of being buried under bills that won't be paid off until next Christmas.
• Actually enjoy the holiday season!

Christmas Quiz

1. Will you send Christmas cards this year? To whom? Relatives and friends in distant areas only, fellow employees, friends and relatives in your own area? What are post office deadlines for the mailing of cards and gifts to other locales?

2. What is the total amount you will be able to spend on gifts this year? How many names will be on your gift list? Will you give token gifts to others such as postman, maintenance man, teachers, colleagues?

3. Will you host a holiday party this year? If so, what is your budget and how many guests will you invite?

4. Will you go away for the holidays? If so, you must decide on a destination, arrange for tickets, set aside money for your trip, decide on whether or not you will also send holiday cards and give Christmas presents. If so, when? Will you buy them on your trip or before, mail cards from your destination or before you leave?

5. Do you plan to have a tree this year? Will you buy it at a local outlet or cut it yourself at a Christmas tree farm? If the latter, you may need to reserve a tree well in advance. Will you hold a tree decorating party? Will you host a children's party?

6. Will Christmas dinner this year be just family or will you also invite relatives and friends? What will you serve? What is your budget?

7. What kind of Christmas do you want for yourself this year? If you are married, this should be decided at a family meeting in October or early November and appropriate plans made.

8. Single and planning to entertain? You may want to consider sharing hostess duties and expenses with one or two friends. Will you need to buy special decorative holiday items, what type of party will it be, what is your holiday food and decorating budget?

9. Will you plan special charitable events, donations or volunteer work this year, such as a visit to a nursing home, offer your services to package holiday items for the needy, donate money or supplies to the homeless? Will you include your children? If single, can you allocate volunteer time outside of working hours for worthy causes?

10. What church activities do you plan? Will you attend services on Christmas Eve, Christmas Day? Sing in the choir? Help with decorations? Serve on a committee?

2.

That Holiday Budget

Have you ever faced Christmas, wondering where the money was coming from to buy cards, gifts, holiday decorations, even your Christmas tree?

If you're like most of us, that scenario is a familiar one. It's easy to avoid thoughts of the holiday season until it is actually upon us—too late to budget a monthly amount to ensure enough money for Christmas.

Decide now that you will plan ahead for next Christmas. Not only will a plan allow you to feel in control, you will be ahead financially as well.

One solution that appeals to many is to open a Christmas Club account with a local bank. In this, you decide how much you will deposit each month, collecting the proceeds in time for shopping in the Fall. Some opt for a payroll savings deduction plan, so the money is not missed when the paycheck arrives.

Others decide to use a passbook savings account to save money for the Santa season. Each month, a variable amount is placed into the account, which then collects interest.

If you do this, decide on a minimum amount you will save each month, but add more to this, if possible. Do not use this account for anything other than Christmas expenses. Use the money in this account each month when you purchase your gifts ahead of time.

If you decide to open a Christmas Club account, and yet would like to do your Christmas shopping throughout the year instead of waiting for Fall, that can also be done.

You might consider charging your purchases each month, carefully keeping track of the totals on the Gift Record form at the back of this book. In Fall when you receive the proceeds from the Christmas Club you can either pay off all the charges made during the year, or if you have been paying your account in full each month, use this windfall sum beginning next year for that year's holiday gifts.

To estimate how much you will actually need, use the Christmas Budget form at the end of this chapter. Divide the total expenses by 12 to find monthly amount you will need to set aside.

Try These Money Saving Ideas

1. Exchange babysitting time with a neighbor.

2. Try to always shop the sales when buying your Christmas gifts.

3. Share holiday dinner with another family, other singles, or relatives. Each brings a portion of the dinner.

4. Set realistic limits on gifts. Do not exceed them, no matter what the temptation. Let your children know in advance what these limits are.

5. If you have many presents to buy for a large group of relatives, consider exchanging names with other family members so you don't have to buy for each person.

6. Entertain friends this year at a holiday brunch or afternoon tea instead of full buffet or sit-down dinner.

7. Instead of buying something for each member of a family with whom you exchange gifts, try a group present such as a family game.

8. Avoid having packages wrapped at department stores. Prices can often be over $5 to wrap one gift. If free "store wrap" is available, however, take advantage of this service.

9. When you buy gifts that must be mailed, be sure to consider the weight and size of the gift. A large gift can add many dollars in postage fees.

10. Give gifts of service (see Chapter Four, When is a Card a Gift?).

Make a Plan—and Stick to It

Once you have decided upon ways to save for the holidays, use your Christmas Countdown Calendar (Chapter Fourteen) to plan your monthly purchases.

Now is the time, if you have not already done so, to fill out the Gift Profile sheet in your workbook for each important person on your holiday list. When you are shopping, tuck this book in your purse and take it along to remind you of sizes, colors, likes and dislikes.

Always buy at sales, if possible. The end-of-December sale on Christmas cards, gift wrap, ribbons and tags is a "must," and can save you a considerable amount of money.

Record your purchases on your Gift Record form (see Holiday Worksheets), so you have a running tab on how much you have spent and for whom gifts have been purchased. Use this Christmas Gift Checklist to help you recall for whom you must buy gifts.

Christmas Gift Checklist

This Christmas I plan to buy gifts for the following people: (Place check marks after names)

Husband	Wife	Cousin
Son	Daughter	Sister-in-law
Mother	Father	Brother-in-law
Grandmother	Grandfather	Mother-in-law
Sister	Brother	Father-in-law
Aunt	Uncle	Grandchildren
Niece	Nephew	Newspaper person
Colleagues	Teacher	Sports associates
Dentist	Doctor	Attorney
Chiropractor	Postman	Beautician
Veterinarian	Doorman	Maintenance person

Before You Shop

Decide how much you will spend today and for whom you will shop. Bring along a pen, eyeglasses, if you wear them; tape measure and your Holiday Handbook. You will need to refer to your Gift Profile sheets.

Check in advance on store hours of the shops you plan to visit, as well as their layaway and return policies. Do they take credit cards? Personal checks? Is there enough parking?

Wear comfortable clothing, and most of all, shoes you can walk in for hours. Plan to take breaks during the time you are there; have a cup of coffee, tea or a soft drink at a coffee shop or nearby restaurant.

If you have children, do consider shopping alone, even if you must hire a babysitter. Some shopping malls offer child-care facilities, so that is a possibility.

It's difficult to concentrate on shopping, getting a bargain that's truly a bargain, finding the right gift for the right person, if children are tugging you constantly in another direction. Plan another special day when you can shop with them and help them purchase their own gifts.

When is a Bargain not a Bargain?

It's exciting to find offerings at special prices, but some bargains are better left on the sale tables. Even if the item is sale priced, perhaps that figure is so high that it throws your budget out of kilter—don't buy it!

If the merchandise is soiled or damaged, the recipient of your gift will feel he or she is also second-rate in your eyes.

Some bargain items are obviously very much out of date and out of style. It's one thing to buy something for yourself that you might wear anyway, but your friend Elizabeth will be very much aware that what she is receiving is an end-of-the-season sale gift.

Where to Shop
Department stores are the obvious place for many of us, but there are other less traditional outlets that can offer unusual gifts.

If you plan to shop at a variety of firms, do plan your shopping trip with an economical use of time.

Plan to combine all gift buying to be done at the sporting goods store, for instance, in one trip. On another day, you can buy gifts at the bookstore for those on your list who would enjoy a gift from this source.

Interesting Places to Shop for Gifts
Try the museum gift shop, an art supply firm, bookstore, antique shop, beauty supply firm, hardware store, sporting goods firm, florist, automotive supply store, bath boutique, jewelry store, pipe and smoke shop, health food firm, delicatessen, plant nursery, bank (a fine buy is a U.S. Savings Bond), dance wear outlet, off-price family department store such as Marshalls and Ross, toy store, greeting card shop, luggage firm, drug store, factory outlet, kitchenware supply firm, local Christian book store/gift shop, shoe store, college bookstore, garage sale, pet shop, furniture store, record store or music supply shop, senior handicraft center in your town, church bazaar, office supply firm, flea market, candy store, hospital gift shop, photo equipment store, travel agency, video store—and even your local post office where you can buy mint blocks of stamps and catalogs to hold them.

Using Credit
That is the operative phrase. Don't let it use you!

Do review your credit card statements. Decide how much more you can afford to charge, before you even leave home. In addition, decide well in advance how much you will charge during that month.

You might also want to figure out how much interest you'll pay. Would it be better to pay cash for a less expensive gift instead?

Carry only credit cards with you for the stores at which you plan to shop. If possible, put all purchases on one card. That way, you'll realize how much you're adding on. If you charge on several cards, it's too easy to believe that you're not spending much simply because the total on each card is small.

As you record gifts bought on your Gift Record sheet, note whether you paid cash or charged it. Sometimes it's easy to just tuck a charge slip into a file folder or dresser drawer and forget how much was actually spent.

Consider paying off your charge account, if possible, as soon as you get your statement, saving you considerable interest. In some cases, you will pay no interest at all, if the account is paid in full within a specified time.

Call the "800" number listed on your credit card account immediately if your card is stolen. Don't let someone else do their Christmas shopping using your card!

Now You're Ready . . .

. . . to face the Christmas holidays knowing a plan has been created that takes into account your financial situation. No more will you face the new year burdened with bills for Christmas gifts that may already be forgotten.

Money is never the key to a truly happy Christmas. Thoughtfulness makes the leanest holiday glow with enjoyment, a pleasure that does not require $$ signs to make it a special occasion.

Planning is not a restriction. Instead, it frees you to have the kind of Christmas that is not only affordable, but takes into consideration the people on your Christmas list—their desires, hopes, pleasures, hobbies, interests and activities.

It's impossible to lose when you provide that kind of day for those whom you love!

YOUR CHRISTMAS BUDGET

ITEM	EST. COST
1. Gifts for _____ people (Transfer total from Holiday Gift worksheet)	_____
2. Christmas tree	_____
3. Holiday decorations/linens/towels	_____
4. Christmas cards	_____
5. Postage for cards and packages	_____
6. Photos and film	_____
7. Holiday entertaining	_____
Food	_____
Beverages	_____
Invitations	_____
Catering/serving help	_____
New clothing	_____
8. Holiday travel expenses	_____
9. Gift wrapping paper, tags, ribbon	_____
10. Holiday shopping expenses (bridge toll, parking, lunch or dinner out)	_____
11. Other expenses	_____

NOTE: Decide now to open a Christmas Club or other savings account in the new year. Plan how much you can save each month, and pay this amount into your account each year as if it were a bill you owed.

Enter amount you plan to save each month here:

$_____

3.

Christmas Cards—Keeping in Touch

One of life's special moments comes when you open your mailbox to find a Christmas card from a friend you haven't seen in some time. Inside the card, there is a newsy letter that fills you in on what has been happening in her life; perhaps even a photo.

Suddenly, for a few brief moments, your cares are gone and you have drifted backward in time to sunny days shared, laughter and tears, pages in the scrapbook of your life.

Her letter lets you add present events to your shared past, increasing the bonds that tie you together.

For many of us, that Christmas card and letter may be the only contact we have with distant friends, and yet the task of buying, addressing, stamping and mailing cards, as well as writing personal notes on each, becomes an ominously difficult one as Christmas nears.

Nevertheless, it's a link to the past we are reluctant to sever, so we continue this special custom, despite our busy schedules.

Here are ways designed to help you make this often tedious task both less burdensome and more pleasant.

Sending Cards This Year? Here's Help!

1. Trim your card list! Consider sending only to friends and relatives in distant locales, those you see rarely during the year. Try to keep the number of names under 50.

2. Take time to create a new Christmas card file, using the pages at the end of this book. If you haven't received a card from friends for the past two years, drop their name from your list. (If they missed one year, perhaps they were on vacation—give them another year).

3. Haven't received a card from a friend in some time? If the friendship has been a close one, and distance precludes a personal visit, try writing a brief postcard in January, when you have more leisure time. Perhaps there has been an illness in the family, or other events made it difficult to write during the holidays.

4. Decide next year to purchase your cards in late December or early January for the following year. You will find discounts of 50 percent or more.

If you missed that opportunity this year, purchase your cards this Fall as soon as they are on the racks in your favorite store while selection is at its peak. At the beginning of the season, some shops may even offer free engraving, or two-for-one specials.

5. If your list is extensive and can't be trimmed any further, consider the postcard greeting. You might have one created with a photo of you or your family on the reverse side. In addition to reduced postage, there are no gummed flaps to lick or envelopes to stuff, and "white space" for writing is limited, so you won't be tempted to write more than you have time for.

6. If it is important to impart considerable information, such as a change of address, travel plans, or the arrival of a new baby, consider composing a Christmas letter, to be printed at your local quick-print shop. If you use decorative art work (photos can also be incorporated), you need not send a card. (See Chapter Five "Writing the Christmas Letter).

7. If you are married, enlist the help of your family in addressing cards. Elementary, junior high and high school students often have fine penmanship. Younger children will also feel they are regarded as an important part of the family's holiday preparations when you involve them in tasks they can see are very necessary.

8. If you are single, try to set aside two evenings each week in November to write your cards, until your list is complete. Invite a friend over and address cards together. Even if the work doesn't actually go more quickly, it seems to.

9. If you have limited your card list to those you see rarely during the year, or if you have chosen to have your name imprinted on your cards, do write a brief personal note on each card. Otherwise, your greeting appears much too stiff, formal and impersonal, the last impression you wish to give during such a happy season.

10. If you have chosen not to enclose a pre-printed letter, and the task of writing personal notes on each card seems formidable, try this:

Compose a brief personal note no longer than three paragraphs which includes the most pertinent information you'd like to impart to friends—and copy this note on each card, changing only the salutation. Add a personal postscript, if you wish.

You may end up writing just as much, but the task will be easier because you won't have to compose anew the information to be penned on each card.

11. Consider having a favorite photo mass-printed at your local quick-print shop, and include one with each card to close friends or relatives. The cost is usually much less than having photo cards printed, and more individual.

12. Having photo greeting cards printed? Remember to order these early enough! In addition, if you order far enough in advance, a size-able discount may be possible.

However, when sending this type of card, you must realize it is not appropriate for every name on your list. Do NOT send to casual acquaintances or business connections. For these people, do purchase a supply of attractive but more conventional cards.

13. Remember, just because you receive a card does not mean that you have to reciprocate. If you mail a card and it is received after Christmas, your recipient will realize it was obviously an after-thought. Consider writing a brief note or mailing a New Year's greeting instead.

14. Do mail early enough to be sure that recipients who live in distant areas receive their cards on time. Many post office officials advise mailing such cards by the last week in November.

15. Avoid the obviously trendy, bizarre or overly humorous cards, which might offend those who receive them, unless you are very sure of the recipient's taste.

Consider the Tastes of Others

When choosing cards, you may wish to select two varieties, to suit different people on your Christmas list. It's easy to guess that some might be offended by a scene depicting Santa Claus coming to town on a surfboard, or modernistic designs that leave out traditional symbols.

However, if you have friends whose tastes also run to a surfing Santa, and that reflects you and your interests, send them this card. For others on your list, choose any design that they may find more in keeping with the season, such as the Three Wise Men on their camels, a manger scene, the star of Bethlehem, a firelit hearthside or a snow bedecked countryside.

This is not ignoring who you are, but showing consideration for the tastes of others, in the true spirit of the season.

Above all, remember that the friends to whom you send cards are actually receiving a visit from you, so choose or create ones that reflect your own personality, and yet respect the deep feelings of others.

Speaking of Signatures . . .

Few hard and fast rules on anything exist today, but there are certain traditions that often make life a bit less complicated. If you are sending cards this year, you may wonder about appropriate signatures.

If you are single, simply use your full name (Linda Stewart or Jeff Hardisty, for instance), unless cards are only for relatives or friends who will identify you unmistakably by your first name. But unless it's Heloise or Zsa-Zsa, you may be surprised to discover the recipient may not be really certain who the sender is!

As a couple (Linda and Jeff, for example), it's best to precede the two first names with "The Hardistys," and on the line below, list the two given names, Jeff and Linda.

For a more formal signature, use Jeff and Linda Hardisty.

If you decide to use only first names on the card—and this is not recommended—do at least put your full name and address on the envelope. Remember, your friends may know other Linda's and Jeff's.

For a family, it's perhaps easiest to write "The Hardistys" on the top line, followed underneath by Jeff, Linda, Pam and Greg.

If the task of signing the cards falls to you, your name comes last. Remember, if you prefer, cards may be both signed and addressed using colored ink. It's just a matter of your own personal taste.

Also, when you are addressing cards to those on your list with families, do not put "and family" on the envelope. Address the card to the parents, although you may wish to add a note to the children on the inside.

For women using a hyphenated name when they are married, try signing the card, "Jeff Hardisty and Linda Stewart-Hardisty."

Having Your Cards Engraved?

Having your cards engraved? Some people prefer to engrave both name and message formally: "Mr. and Mrs. Jeffrey Hardisty wish you a Merry Christmas."

If you are more informal, have your names printed "Linda and Jeffrey Hardisty." You can include the children's names, although it's preferable to do this only on cards to personal friends.

Should you decide to do this, the husband's name would come first: Jeffrey and Linda Hardisty, Pam and Greg.

. . . And Now, in Closing

Many closing lines are possible on cards. These include:

Affectionately, Warmly, As ever, Fondly, Wishing you peace and joy in the New Year, Wishing you happiness always, Best wishes for a happy holiday season, Joyfully yours, Hoping to see you soon—or even more simply, Love, a sentiment that is never inappropriate.

Special Consideration

When sending a card to a friend or relative who has been bereaved during the past year, you will want to make sure that any card, as well as its message, reflects an emphasis on the spiritual meaning of the season rather than the merriment of the holidays. That first Christmas can be extremely difficult.

Your friend will definitely appreciate any personal message you find time to add to your card, also, such as "Jeff and I send you our very best this holiday season. I know this has been a difficult time for you, but you have our love, prayers and wishes for a better year ahead. Jeff and Linda."

If someone you care about has been hospitalized, take a card and special gift in person, if possible, with a promise to write a brief card each day until they are able to go home.

If you keep a supply of postcards you have already stamped in your stationery drawer, this task can take a maximum of five minutes.

Addressing Cards

When writing your cards, be sure the addresses are legible. If your handwriting is not known for its neatness, consider printing the recipient's name and address. Do not write in pencil, or in ink that is so pale or faint as to be difficult to read.

Your card is an investment in time and energy, and it would be a shame for it to go astray because the postman was unable to decipher the address.

It's worthwhile to invest in return address labels or an address stamp before the holidays. That way, the job of putting your own return address on cards is reduced to simply placing labels on or stamping the envelopes.

It is very necessary to place a return address on cards for two reasons. First, you will want to know if the card you sent actually arrived at its destination. "Moved: Left No Forwarding Address" at least lets you know you can take that name off your card list!

Second, if anything is wrong with the piece you mailed—insufficient postage, for instance—the post office will have no way of knowing where to return the card, and you will be left assuming it reached its destination.

Mailing Your Christmas Cards

According to many post office officials, cards should be in the mail the last week in November, if they are being sent out of state, or by the first week in December if you are mailing within your state.

It is possible that if you mail later, your cards will still reach their destination in time, but you cannot be certain.

Do keep in mind that pieces of mail which do not meet the following requirements may not be mailed through the United States Post Office:

Your letter or card must be at least .007 of an inch thick, must be rectangular in shape, at least 3 1/2 inches high and at least 5 inches long.

Mail that is more than 1/4 inch thick can be mailed, however, even if it measures less than 3 1/2 by 5 inches.

Reminders

1. Set aside enough time to create or buy your cards, address, stamp and mail them. Include time to write personal notes or a holiday letter. Allow extra time if you are having photos made or letters printed for enclosures.

2. If possible, begin no later than the first week in November to buy or create, address and stamp your Christmas cards. If you plan to make your own cards, late summer or early fall is even better. Christmas notes or letters can be added in November, so information is current.

3. Buy your Christmas cards for next year at this year's end-of-December sale, for savings of 50 percent or more.

4. Begin NOW keeping a cardboard box handy for items of interest such as news clippings you may wish to include in Christmas cards. If something interesting happens to you or your family, write it down and toss it in the box. It's all too easy to forget even the highlights in our lives months later.

5. If you are buying cards this year, consider purchasing them from a charitable organization or your local church, or an organization such as UNICEF (for free catalog, write UNICEF, 1 Children's Blvd., Ridgely, MD 21865).

6. Have you decided to stop sending Christmas cards? Do consider sending them this one last year. Enclose a brief note informing your correspondents about your decision and noting any alternative way you or your family may have decided to use the money, such as donations to local charities.

This way, friends and relatives who are used to receiving an annual card won't wonder why they have suddenly been dropped from your list!

Remember That . . .

Whatever you decide to do—send cards, not send them, design them or buy them—the decision is a very personal one that only you can make.

It doesn't matter what your friends and relatives are doing, or what your own family tradition has always been. You alone know what is best for you, so whatever you do, the decision you have made is appropriate. Go ahead, relax—and enjoy the holiday season knowing you have done what is right for you.

4.
When is a Card a Gift?

Consider the possibility of combining Christmas cards and gifts to those who live far away. This keeps you from having to make a separate trip to the post office to mail a bulky and often quite expensive, package.

Remember to have your envelope weighed for correct postage and to insure all valuables sent through the mail. Do not send cash. Since mail is machine-canceled, bulky items should be marked "Hand Cancel."

Easy-to-mail items include:

Personal check, gift certificate, United States Savings Bond, share of stock, book of cinema tickets, mint blocks of current stamps, tickets to an upcoming sporting event, membership in an organization (local historical society, museum, theater group, YMCA, YWCA are all possibilities).

Who wouldn't enjoy theater tickets for two to a play in a nearby city; a book of raffle tickets; coupons to be redeemed for specified services you offer to perform, or a poem you've written, song you've composed or painting you've created just for the recipient?

Always welcome are gift certificates from a favorite department store, sporting goods store or boutique. Also fun to receive and easy to mail might be a lace handkerchief, silk scarf, or coins for a collection.

Consider mailing a card letting the recipient know you have entered a subscription to her hometown newspaper or to his favorite magazine.

A Gift of Love is Never Out of Date

Some of the people on your list are bound to be the ones for whom you throw up your hands in despair and mutter, "He (or she) has got simply everything. There's nothing in the world they need!"

Perhaps not, and yet there are things they would love and appreciate that are not available in stores, gifts that are more appreciated than a diamond from Tiffany's or a new BMW—well, maybe! And anyhow, the following gifts are certainly much easier to mail.

Christmas is for Everyone

Everyone—yes, everyone—needs a gift of love.

Don't buy the platitude that tells you, "Christmas is just for children." Christmas has always been for everyone who knows what it means to give—and to receive. And the older you get, the more it means.

Remember the time you received a gift card from your sister that read, "I promise to do dishes for you on nights when you have a date." Could there have been a more welcome gift?

You'll probably forget by January the gift gloves you received in December, but the gift that keeps on giving is one that lingers in your heart all year long.

The wonderful part about these gifts is, most are free. All they take is time, love and caring, a willingness to share our lives with another.

Try giving a gift of love this year and see the joy it can bring. Here are some to start with, but you can easily create others that will surpass these in pleasure given—and received.

These Gifts are Never Out of Date

1. Offer to house-sit for a friend who is planning a vacation.

2. Present coupons redeemable for a specified number of hours of baby sitting for a friend who has a small child.

3. Give certificates good for one visit each week to an elderly friend or relative in a nursing home.

4. Take a friend to lunch once a month next year.

5. Offer to grocery shop each week for a specified number of months for a shut-in relative. Combine the grocery trip with a personal visit.

6. Promise to take a child on one special occasion trip each month—just the two of you.

7. Take a friend or relative who is unable to get out often, for a Sunday outing or visit to your home.

8. Enclose tickets for a sporting event you know he's been wanting to see—and say you'll go with him!

9. Offer to clean house one afternoon each week for a month for a relative who has been ill, or pay for such a service.

10. Circus coming to town? Offer to take your child and one friend.

11. Volunteer to make one library visit each week for a month for a friend who is ill.

12. Let your gift recipient know that you will visit each Wednesday evening.

13. Enjoy gardening? Offer to provide one month of free garden work, one hour per week.

14. For a colleague at work, offer to bring one special brown bag lunch to work each week—and have lunch together.

15. Offer to give a friend or colleague a ride home for a specified number of times, if transportation is a problem.

16. Do you work a shift schedule? Offer to change shifts an indicated number of times with a fellow worker who needs the change.

17. Walk a friend's dog once a week for a month.

18. Are you a teenage girl with more time than money? Offer to lend your friend your best blouse, a sweater, help with homework, a sympathetic ear when she's had a fight with her boyfriend.

19. Teenage boys often find a shortage of cash around the holidays, too, and yet don't want to forget friends. Why not offer to do your best friend's chores for a week, set him up with that cute new girl in French class, or help him study for that Geometry final?

20. Last, but not least, a gift that is good for any age, anytime, anywhere. Offer a hug and a listening ear anytime it is needed, and your gift will never be forgotten.

5.

Writing the Christmas Letter

One of the most time-consuming tasks of the holiday season can be writing individual notes or letters to each person on your Christmas card list.

You feel obligated to let Aunt Jenny, whom you haven't seen in more than a year, know how you are doing, how your work is coming, and all about the children.

Like many of us, knowing the work that lies ahead, you put it off until early December. At that time, you're probably also busy with tasks at home, giving or attending holiday parties, arranging child care for children home for Christmas vacation or planning activities for them at that time—and last, but not least, finishing your Christmas shopping!

About the last thing you want to do is write dozens of letters. The answer? The printed Christmas letter, general enough to send to everyone, and yet specific enough to let your own personality shine through.

Tips on Writing the Holiday Letter
Here are some tips which will help make composing your letter easier.

1. You must decide initially what size letter you will have printed. The most successful size, and the least expensive, is the 8 1/2 inch by 11 inch, although if you have a great deal of news, the legal size (same width, but a few inches longer) can also work well.

2. Now, decide what art work you will use, where it will go and what space it will require. Perhaps you or one of your children or a friend who is talented at drawing would be willing to sketch holiday bells, poinsettias, a wreath or star or some other symbol of the holidays for you.

3. If this is not possible, consult your local printer or art supply firm for their stock of available holiday "clip art." This is just what its name

implies, clips of suitable holiday artwork that are inexpensive but very attractive. It can raise your letter from simply a grey, printed page to a true holiday greeting, that can even replace a card, if you desire.

In addition, at the holiday season many quick print shops carry a supply of paper with suitable art work already in place. If so, it is as simple as choosing which one you like.

4. Another possibility is including a photo of your family as part of the art work. This is not difficult for your printer to do, and results in a very attractive greeting.

5. Now, create a dummy (mock-up) of your page. This will let you know how much space you will have for your actual letter.

6. You are ready to begin the actual letter now. In this initial draft, write just as you would to a friend, one whom you care about very much but are not trying to impress. Remember, this letter will be going to many people, but you are writing for just one person, that special friend.

7. If you are married and have children, check with each family member at this point to see if there is something special they would like included.

8. After you have received everyone's comments and completed your own draft, you are ready for the final product. Remember, as you read it, that it shouldn't sound like the kind of letter satirized by comedians. You know the type—Jeff is off to West Point, Lynn was valedictorian of her class, and Spot rated top dog in the local show. It's only human to resent, and perhaps be suspicious of, such perfection.

Include your successes, of course, but don't be afraid to share difficulties experienced during the year. Perhaps a parent or grandparent died, or someone whom you are close to was very ill, but is now recovering. Your aim is to present a rounded picture of your life during the year.

Be proud of your accomplishments, but don't be afraid to let friends know it hasn't all been a piece of cake! They'll love you more for sharing.

9. Once you have the final error-free draft of your letter typed on the size paper you have chosen, use rubber cement to paste on the art work. Use a straight edge to make sure art work is not crooked.

10. Now is the time to sign your production. Be sure to have everyone, even the children, add their own signatures. If possible, leave some space at the bottom of the letter. This you may use for a brief personal note to special friends, if desired.

Last But Not Least . . .

Take your production to your local quick-print shop, the earlier the better. When you pick the letters up, check one copy for errors while you are still in the shop. That way, if there is a serious error, you won't have to make another round trip to bring them in for correction.

Once you are sure they are correct, all that now remains to do is fold and insert them in your Christmas cards, or alternatively, buy envelopes for the letters and use them in place of a holiday greeting card.

You have now conquered the "I don't think I can write one more Christmas note!" problem forever—or at least for this year.

6.

How to Select a Gift

One of the special delights of the holiday season is the thrill of watching friends open presents you've carefully selected and seeing their pleasure when they tell you, "How did you know? This is exactly what I wanted!"

Mastering the art of matching the gift to the person takes thought, practice and observation, however. How many times have you received a present from someone only to find that it didn't reflect "you" at all. It was simply generic, a gift for the sake of giving, not one that said "I care about you and know who you are."

Christmas especially finds many of us concerned that what we are about to give may not be received with equal pleasure. There are some guidelines that will help you match the right present to the right person, however. If you follow these suggestions, using your own special thoughtfulness and observation, yours will be the gift under the tree that will be enjoyed for months afterward, not discarded in a closet or drawer.

Gift-giving is actually a matter of really looking at a friend, lover, husband, child or relative, really seeing them, listening to what moves them, observing what they enjoy wearing, hearing their comments about what they like to do, where they like to go, favorite colors, what their hobbies and interests are.

Christmas is love and caring, and your gifts will reflect this seasonal spirit if you follow these easy suggestions.

Choosing the Gift that Says "I Care"

1. Notice his reaction to other gifts in the past. What were his comments when the gift was revealed? Did he express simple politeness, or was real pleasure evident when the package was opened? Was the gift used after the holidays, or stored and forgotten?

2. If you have shopped together, what has caught his eye? Has he mentioned a color, a style, a type of clothing or equipment that he likes?

3. Think about the person's likes and dislikes. Consider hobbies and special interests, the way free time is spent. Does he enjoy movies or backpacking, opera or jazz, picnics in the country or dinner at an elegant restaurant?

4. Try suggesting gifts to your friend during conversation and watch for a reaction. You might say, "Isn't that a great dress? I think you'd look terrific in something red and slinky like that." If her reaction is "Not in a million years. I'm just not that type," then you'll know better than to buy her that rhinestone studded tie you think is so fashionable.

5. Which leads us to the next rule—don't assume your intended recipient will like everything you like. If you love sports and think the best gift in the world is matching headband, socks and shorts, don't decide your bookish friend who loves an evening at the theater will be overjoyed with such a gift. She may simply tuck it in a drawer with venomous thoughts about a friend who gives gifts she herself would like to get!

6. You could have avoided the problem gift in paragraph five had you listened to clues in your conversations. Your friend may rave over the elegant gilded jewelry box she received last year to hold all her earrings, or sigh with exasperation over the gift of a five-pound box of chocolates when all her friends knew she was on a diet. Listen!

7. Don't use a gift as a chance to impress. A fancy gift out of your price range to friends may have an effect opposite to the one you desired. They may feel an expensive gift is an attempt to manipulate, and feel trapped. If they reciprocate in kind, they will be angry. If they don't, they may feel guilty, so that is a lose-lose situation for you.

8. Listen to past memories of gifts your friend or relative has received. If your husband talks nostalgically about the harmonica he got when he was 10, and what fun it would be to take it up again sometime, you've got a clue for a great gift.

Also, listen to complaints about gifts NOT received. Does your friend regret never being given some special item as she was growing up? A pair of lacy gloves, roller skates, her own Monopoly set, a glittery evening bag? It's never too late, and she will always remember your thoughtfulness—and the fact that YOU remembered what she said.

9. Avoid gifts for those close to you that are simply utilitarian. If a spouse needs a new vacuum, she will probably buy one somehow out of household money. If your husband's favorite coffeemaker has just ceased to function, buy him another one—but not for Christmas!

Remember, gifts are special because they are often items your friends would love to have, but wouldn't spend money on for themselves.

10. Vow now not to give one more bottle of cologne, fifth of Scotch, tie or scarf to anyone on your Christmas list this year! Those are easy gifts that all too rarely reflect the taste and needs of the intended recipient.

11. If you do give such a gift, pair it with an imaginative companion. A fine bottle of Greek brandy accompanied by a cut crystal brandy snifter, or a scarf in your friend's favorite color accompanied by eye makeup in coordinating shades.

12. Don't try to improve someone with your gift. A friend who is overweight won't appreciate that diet book or jump rope. Your non-athletic cousin may not enjoy a set of hand weights; and if you have someone on your gift list who thinks reading means checking the TV Guide for a favorite sitcom, a gift of the latest Great American Novel will certainly not be his cup of tea.

Such a gift merely says, "I don't like you the way you are. I wish you would improve." That's not a message you mean to send at Christmas!

13. Rounding off this baker's dozen hints, try your own skills to create meaningful gifts that aren't necessarily expensive. Give a gift of service, baby-sit for a housebound friend, offer an evening of conversation to an older relative who is lonely.

If you are an artist, paint a pastel or small oil for someone special; if you're a writer, create a poem. These gifts and others like them will be treasured forever.

You Can Do It

Most of all, however, learn from your mistakes. We've all given gifts bought in haste and regretted at leisure, but next year things can be different.

Next year, you may want to trim your gift list, perhaps draw names, to create a Christmas within your budgetary and energy bounds.

It's easy to become frustrated when you have to shop for too many presents with too little money, and not enough time to buy creatively.

When Christmas is over this year, sit down, use the guidelines in this book and create a plan which will allow you to be in control. Next year you will give gifts that were a pleasure to shop for, economical to buy and memorable to receive.

7.

Tips For the Last-Minute Shopper

All is not lost if you have waited until the last few days—or even the last day—before Christmas. There are many gifts that can be bought easily and quickly, gifts that are suitable for each person on your list.

If you haven't done so already, your first step will be to make out your Christmas list, using the Holiday Gift List in the Holiday Workbook section, Chapter Fifteen.

Include each person to whom you wish to give a gift—friends, relatives, spouse, children, the postman, newspaper boy, building maintenance man, employer, colleagues, or any others you feel you need to buy for.

Next to each name on this list, write the dollar amount you plan to spend. You might also wish to note one or two gift ideas for each person on this sheet.

In addition, take time now to fill out a Gift Profile Form (also listed in the Holiday Workbook section) for each important person on your list. This will give you a list of your gift recipient's sizes, favorite colors, likes and dislikes to take with you when you shop.

Shopping Tips

The following suggestions are beneficial whether you do your gift shopping early in the season or late in December.

1. When you shop, consider the interests and hobbies of the person you are buying for, and also think about purchasing gifts this year at out-of-the way shops, rather than large department stores.

2. Many interesting items can be bought at antique stores, sporting goods firms, beauty supply houses, bookstores, or even plant nurseries.

3. Try to shop on a weekday when crowds are at a minimum. If that is not possible, why not go immediately after work? Combine your shopping trip with dinner out with a friend, roommate or spouse.

4. Take a large shopping bag with you so you won't have to juggle an armful of small packages.

5. Taking a quick look at the checkout lines at the store in which you are planning to shop can let you know ahead of time what to expect. You might decide to go elsewhere or come back at a less busy time.

6. If you are having your gifts mailed by the store, be sure before you leave home that you have all addresses neatly printed on index cards, easy to give to the clerk at the gift wrap counter.

7. If you park in a large lot at a shopping center, you might want to take a moment to jot down the location of your car. When you've shopped for hours and are tired, it's sometimes hard to remember just where the car was parked.

Shopping Safety Tips

The holiday season, unfortunately, has more than its share of crime. Opportunities for pickpockets and other thieves abound, but there are things you can do to minimize the risk when you are shopping.

1. Keep valuable items in the zippered compartment of your handbag.

2. You are at risk if your arms are full of packages. As your shopping bag fills up, return to the car and put your packages in the trunk—not the car itself, where they are visible and tempting.

3. Carry a bag with shoulder straps, so your hands are free.

4. When you park your car, choose a parking space under a light, as close to the store as possible. Do not park next to vans and trucks which can make it easy for someone to hide.

5. Have your car keys ready when you leave the store for your car, and look around to make sure no one is near when you get in.

6. If you feel someone is following you, return to the store. This is always a case where it's better to be safe than sorry.

7. Check the back seat of the car before you get in, and lock the door immediately after you. Do not leave it open while you sort your packages.

Last Minute Gift Ideas

Why not go to a bank and buy a $50 savings bond for each important person on your list? The bonds are currently a fine investment. Each $50 bond costs you only $25, and your entire list, including relatives, friends and even children can be taken care of in one trip to your local bank.

If you would like a more personalized gift, give a certificate good for a service dear to the heart of each person on your list.

With a few phone calls, you can arrange for certificates for an astrological reading, relaxing massage, a facial, manicure and pedicure, a series of aerobic classes, or tennis, racquetball or golfing lessons.

Many memberships in local organizations are very inexpensive and offer lasting benefits throughout the year. What about enrolling someone on your gift list in the local historical society, arts guild, Audubon group, YMCA or YWCA, theater organization, writing group, woman's club, or other specialized groups?

Another unusual but gratifying gift would be tickets to a popular play in the nearest city (if this is for an older single adult, perhaps add a note that you will be accompanying her or him on the trip).

A similar gift idea would be a book of tickets to the nearest cinema, gift certificate at a favorite local restaurant for a specified number of meals, or tickets to sporting events you know the recipient would like to attend.

What about a paid enrollment in a spring class at a local community college you know your friend would enjoy? Classes can cost as little as $5 at many colleges.

Gift certificates from a hobby shop, sporting goods firm, department store or beauty supply firm are less unusual but always welcome.

What about gifts of elegant stationery for everyone on your list, with a book of first-class postage stamps enclosed?

Buy potpourri in bulk at your local herb store and spend one evening making sachets of satin tied with varied colors of ribbon and decorated with silk flowers. Tuck each potpourri sachet in with an elegant guest towel and scented soap.

Buy an assortment of dried fruits, nuts and cheese at your local health food store and arrange attractively in baskets you have purchased at your local import store.

If you know the literary tastes of each person on your gift list, one stop at your local book store can take care of Christmas for everyone, including children.

Don't forget magazine subscriptions. There are many specialized magazines available today, one for every hobby and profession. A simple visit to your magazine stand to purchase the latest copy of each will do it.

Tear out the subscription form and mail with a check to the magazine. Be sure to note that this is a Christmas gift. The magazine itself you will present gift-wrapped on Christmas day, with a note from you that it will be coming all year long as your special gift.

8.

Hostess Gifts and Stocking Stuffers

The holiday season includes perhaps more than half of the parties we attend during the year. Thoughtful partygoers will take along a gift for the hostess, but often we are caught in a last minute flurry of activity only to rush to our nearest liquor store or supermarket for a bottle of wine as our gift.

However, there are gifts you can keep on hand that not only will keep you from having to shop at the last minute, but will mark you as a thoughtful guest indeed.

In addition, don't forget that each of these also makes a thoughtful last-minute gift for a friend.

Hostess Gift Tips

1. Keep a supply on hand of small decorative tins purchased at your import store. They can be used to package everything from nuts and home-baked goodies to guest soaps.

2. Some Sunday afternoon, bake a supply of small loaves of nut and/or fruit bread, wrap in foil and freeze. They are easy to bake, delicious and decorative, and particularly welcome at the holidays.

3. For dog or cat lovers, give your host and hostess a small carved figure of their favorite breed.

4. Why not take a Polaroid picture of each of your best friends, their homes or their pets during the year, (supposedly for your scrapbook, if they ask), and frame in a small silver frame for a very thoughtful and unusual hostess gift or prized Christmas present.

5. Do they collect a certain item? Some people collect replicas of their sun sign, others love cats, or dolphins or unicorns. Whatever the item, you can find it in some inexpensive version, marking you as a thoughtful guest par extraordinaire.

6. Buy a huge sack of your favorite nut in the shell, such as pistachio or almond, and divide into small tins to keep on hand for

guests who drop in over the holidays. The remainder you can use in baking or as nibblers for the family or friends.

7. Decorate your home with a half dozen or more poinsettia plants. Inexpensive at the supermarket, they make lovely holiday appointments until you need one for a hostess gift.

8. Buy a case of wine with your name imprinted (Windsor Vineyards, P.O. Box 368, Windsor, CA 95492-9989). Even this traditional gift seems somehow more special this way. Surprisingly inexpensive!

9. How about fancy stirrers for drinks together with holiday cocktail napkins?

10. Miniature guest soaps in assorted shapes and colors are always welcome gifts for the holiday hostess.

11. Potpourri tied in a red satin square and fastened with a satin ribbon, set off by a sprig of holly is easy to make (buy the potpourri in bulk at your local herb store).

12. Packets of unusual herbs and spices, as well as live herb plants are welcome gifts for the cook.

13. Next year's calendar—for her kitchen.

14. Your favorite recipe, accompanied by a gift-wrapped sample.

15. Buy several pairs of attractive holiday mugs if you see a pre-season sale. They make welcome gifts for the host and hostess.

16. Jars of preserves you have either made yourself or bought at a holiday bazaar. With pinking scissors, cut a round circle of calico fabric for a sunbonnet top. Attach to jar with rubber band or yarn.

17. Ornamental tins packed with gourmet coffee, tea, herbs or candies.

18. Gourmet olive oil packed in small wicker basket with packet of fresh pasta.

19. Jar of homemade salad dressing—with recipe.

20. Basket of fresh seasonal fruits.

Notes on Stocking Stuffers

Many of the items listed both above and below can also serve as gifts for acquaintances, your children's teachers, the postman, maintenance man, colleagues at the office, or anyone who catches you by surprise with a gift, and for whom you have none in return.

It is not necessary to respond in kind to such a surprise gift, but there are times when you simply don't want to hurt someone's feelings. It's nice to have a few of these gifts on hand, already wrapped, for such small emergency situations.

For the Men in Your Life
1. Key chain with fold-up knife
2. Easy-to-read playing cards
3. Indoor/outdoor thermometer
4. Mini lint brush
5. Travel chess or backgammon set
6. Festive bow tie
7. Mini picture frame—with your picture in it
8. Exercise jump rope
9. Set of dominos
10. New shoelaces for his running shoes
11. Lunchtime treats to keep in his desk at work
12. Great coffee beans
13. Bar of fine soap
14. Money clip
15. Silver business card holder

For the Women in Your Life
1. Sachet and scented shelf lining paper
2. Keychain with flashlight
3. Brocade credit card case or eyeglass holder
4. Elegant notecards, pen and stamps
5. Lace handkerchief
6. Vinyl paper clips and desk organizer
7. Make-up mirror for handbag
8. Herbal tea bags
9. Loofah sponge
10. Small sketchbook and mini set of pastels
11. Tea strainer
12. One-cup coffee maker
13. Desk calendar for her office
14. Set of make-up brushes
15. Set of bookplates

Holiday Tipping Guidelines
An unexpected expense at the end of the year can be holiday tipping. What to give the postman, newspaper delivery boy, or janitor in your building is a question most of us have asked.

The answer is to tip those with whom you have regular contact. If you have been satisfied with their service throughout the year, tip—but only what you can afford.

If you're wondering what the gift and/or Christmas card policy is in your new job, ask an employee who has been there some time.

New in the neighborhood? Check gift policies with residents who have lived there longer to find out what is expected, and the kind of tip or gift most often given. If you have only lived there a brief time, tip in proportion to the time you have been a resident.

Neighbors occasionally get together, chipping in to buy a gift for the postman on the route or the apartment building manager.

Inexpensive gifts of food such as preserves, fruitcake, and other holiday baked goods you have purchased at a church bazaar or made yourself are always appropriate. They can be given to your hair-dresser, your children's teachers, fellow employees or acquaintances whom you would like to remember.

Holiday Card or Gift Check List

When you're sending Christmas cards or remembering someone who has rendered fine service to you or your family throughout the year, use this checklist. Note whether you plan to send a card or give a small gift.

People I Would Like to Remember

Fellow employees	Veterinarian
Employer	Sports associates
Attorney	Postman
Fellow club member	Newspaper delivery boy
Club officer	Building superintendent
Doctor	Maintenance man
Teacher(s)	Dentist
Beautician	Doorman

Tahiti, Here I Come!

Christmas at the last minute doesn't have to be an impossible situation. Using the tips in this book, you can avoid those crowded department stores, and that fight for the last available parking place less than six blocks from the shop.

That desperate desire you've had in seasons past to wake up and find yourself basking in the sun in Tahiti, not frantically scurrying around shopping for last-minute items may just disappear.

Although, on second thought, Tahiti doesn't sound bad—maybe next year?

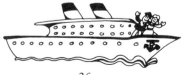

9.
Creating the Gift Basket

If there is someone very special on your list, for whom a single gift somehow just doesn't seem enough, try creating a basket gift. This is one in which you place several related items into a single container, creating a "theme" gift.

Although this gift is almost always more expensive, it nevertheless is one that will be remembered for a long time for the singular thoughtfulness evident in such a present.

A few of the following clustered gifts are too costly for more than the closest friend or relative, but remember—you can create many similar gifts less expensively by substituting low-cost items with a single theme.

Some of the gifts included in the basket ideas listed below can be found in catalogs. Addresses for these firms are listed in Chapter Eleven (Shopping by Mail).

However, if time precludes sending for gifts by mail order this year, similar items are frequently available at specialty stores in most larger cities.

Go ahead—give holiday "basketing" a try!

Wrap Up a Holiday Basket Gift

BIRDWATCHER ▪ Pack a field guide to birds in your area, along with warm gloves and scarf in his/her favorite color. Tuck everything into a large red bandana, tied onto a stick, hobo-style.

ASTROLOGY BUFF ▪ Tuck a pin reflecting her sun sign and a paperback book with her horoscope for the coming year into an inexpensive star-patterned bowl you've purchased at a variety store.

NATURE LOVER ▪ Put a large homespun napkin into a small, rustic basket. Fill with small jars of homemade preserves you've purchased at a church bazaar or made yourself. Nice additions are a small loaf of home-made or bakery fruit-and-nut bread and inexpensive spreading knife.

TEA ENTHUSIAST ▪ Pack a variety of loose teas in small tin canisters from your local import store, labeling each. Add a china cup and saucer, lemon slice squeezer and paperback book on tea preparation. Tuck all into a large white basket lined with rose tissue paper and add a festive bow of silver on the handle.

JUST MARRIED ▪ Pack a bread box from the variety store with all the essentials for beginning housekeeping. Include set of measuring cups and spoons, nested oven-safe bowls, set of wooden cooking spoons, corkscrew for wine, and small packets of dried mixes such as soup, gravy, salad dressing, tea. Include egg timer, jar opener and kitchen scissors, if you wish. To wrap? Just tie a wide red satin ribbon around the box!

LOVE ENTERTAINING? ▪ Pack an elegant ice bucket with bar stockers, stirrers, ice tongs and bottle of his favorite fine liquor. Other possibilities: Crystal champagne cooler with bottle of her favorite champagne and two tulip glasses; or two silver liqueur glasses on small mirrored tray, with bottle of elegant liqueur.

NEW HOMEOWNER ▪ Pack a large metal toolbox with hammer, set of screwdrivers, flashlight, wrench, nails and picture hangers in assorted sizes. Nice additions: Pack of sandpaper in different grades, retractable tape measure, pocket guide for the handyman.

FOR THE READER ▪ Sterling silver bookmark accompanied by latest best-seller, packed with tapestry eyeglass case (if your reader wears glasses). Tuck all into basket lined with latest issue of New York Times.

SPORTS ENTHUSIAST ▪ Matching headband, wristband and athletic socks rolled up in a big, bright terry towel and tucked into a new athletic bag. Add a combination lock and small hair dryer, for those nice extras.

HEALTH NUT ▪ Subscription to Prevention Magazine (Emmaus, PA 18098-0002); assortment of trail mix, granola, raw nuts, and variety of flours and grains packed in quart canning jars. Anyone who is serious about health and food would also enjoy a holiday gift package from Walnut Acres (see listing in Shop By Mail).

UNDER STRESS? ▪ Give a selection from Solitudes or Environments, which re-creates the sounds of nature to soothe, satisfy and relax a harried friend or spouse. (Send for Eddie Bauer catalog, P.O. Box 3700, Seattle, WA 98124).

CHEESE LOVER ▪ Pack cheese slicer and cheese board in large basket. Tuck in several bars of imported cheeses and add stone ground crackers. Nice touch: a bottle of Pinot Noir or Chardonnay from the Sonoma Valley Wine Country. Nice to add: Cheese of All Nations catalog (see "Food" listing in Shop by Mail).

Looking for low-fat, low-sodium cheese? Send for a catalog from Fi-gi's, Inc., 630 S. Central Ave., Marshfield, WI 54449. They also ship fruit boxes.

RUNNERS ▪ Stopwatch with nylon cord and portable foot mas-sager wrapped in sports pages of your local newspaper. Tie package with colored shoelaces.

HANDYMAN ▪ Portable workbench (under $40) by Black and Decker; or a gift certificate from Brookstone (see listing in Shop by Mail). Pack gift certificate in large, two-tier tool kit, wrapped in burlap and tied with twine.

NEW PARENTS ▪ Pack travel tote bag with boxes of baby cereal, teething ring, jars of baby food, stainless spoon, teething biscuits, bibs and travel toys.

DOG LOVER ▪ Give man's best friend a large, chrome pet bowl in which you have placed a rawhide bone, pet toy and box of animal treats.

CAT FANCIER ▪ A catnip toy, grooming comb, pet placemat and new feeding dish would be a hit with your feline friend. Tuck all into a new wicker cat bed.

PASTA FREAK ▪ Put all the ingredients for a special Italian dinner into a copper colander. Add your own recipe for spaghetti sauce or fettucini and include it with small bottle of Extra Virgin olive oil, packet of bread sticks and hard wedge of Romano cheese.

BAKING IS HER HOBBY ▪ She may not have Vienna glass cookie stamps ($6), a pizzelle iron to make crisp Italian wafer cookies ($15), or a heavy tinned steel Madeleine plaque ($12.50) from France to cre-ate the small buttery sponge cakes that melt in your mouth. You can discover a world of items for the dedicated cook by sending for a free catalog from Williams-Sonoma.

Place her gifts, including an oven mitt and two of your own favorite recipes in an inexpensive bread loaf tin. Wrap in aluminum foil and tie with silver yarn to which you have attached a set of measuring spoons.

FOR THE BATH ▪ Buy an across-the-tub shelf that features a mirror and holders for her cosmetics. Add travel-size packet of shampoo, conditioner, luxury cake of soap and her favorite bath oil.

IS CHINESE HER FAVORITE? ▪ Shop at your favorite import store and buy her a 24-piece set of Cantonese dinnerware (under $35). Tuck in chopsticks, a tin of jasmine tea, fortune cookies and a small teapot. Wrap in Oriental gift wrap, available at most import stores. Tape an inexpensive accordion-pleated fan on top of box.

COFFEE DRINKER ▪ Pottery mug inscribed with name; one pound

of high-grade coffee beans, coffee grinder and/or Chambord French press (for great infusion-brewed coffee). Wrap all in large ivory-colored basket, with gifts tucked in brown tissue paper. Buy one coffee-colored napkin and cover top of basket. Add brown satin bow. Nice additions: individual tins of flavored coffees, small cream pitcher and/or sugar bowl.

COOKERY, MEXICAN-STYLE ▪ Try gifts such as a nacho skillet, set of four chili bowls, sangria pitcher, terracotta taco rack or tostada platter (under $20 each). Add Diana Kennedy's "Cuisines of Mexico" cookbook and a tortilla basket fryer (under $15). Tuck in two bottles of Dos Equis beer, and wrap in large cardboard box in brightly colored paper, or inexpensive Mexican scarf.

FOR THE DIETER ▪ Pocket calorie counter, food scale, and diary to record her progress. Add a cookbook featuring gourmet recipes for the dieter. Wrap gift using tape measure as gift tie.

GARDENER ▪ Gardening knee pads (under $20, Brookstone), wildflower seeds (under $2 per pack), and backyard bubbler (under $15). Pack all in garden tool organizer (under $9). All items except knee pads from Holst, Inc.

JAPANESE COOKERY CHARM HER? ▪ Choose a traditional round bottom wok set, which includes tempura rack, spatula, ladle and other utensils. Add a bottle of Kikkoman soy sauce and rice vinegar, and you've got a recipe for a delighted cook. Tuck all gifts in large wicker basket, add small Oriental paper lantern to handle.

OFFICE WORKER (Female) ▪ Travel-size cosmetics, small sewing kit, packet of safety pins, small mirror, scissors, packed in small brocade bag.

OFFICE WORKER (Male) ▪ No-spill auto mug (for the commuter), lint brush, small quartz desk clock or travel-size electric razor, along with mini-size vial of his favorite after-shave lotion. Package all in small leather carrying case.

AN OLDER RELATIVE ▪ Warm flannel sheets in pastels and plaids with matching pillowcases. For a note of luxury, add a 15-way massager/heater adjustable to fit her back (Under $70 from Hammacher-Schlemmer).

Add an electric candle lamp to ensure safety in hallways, bedrooms and light her way to bed (Hanover House, under $10). Wrap all in smallest size wicker trunk, adding useful storage as well as attractive packaging. Add a huge red bow, and your grandmother or aunt will always remember this gift!

OUTDOORSMAN ▪ Sunglasses, waterproof flashlight, water resistant portable radio, tanning lotion with a sun protection factor of

15, plus packs of freeze-dried supplies and a space blanket. Pack all in fishing creel. Great extra? Add a miniature flare gun for under $35 from Sporting Edge.

QUILTER ▪ Save fabric scraps throughout the year from your own sewing projects for a quilting friend. Place patches, cut into four by four-inch squares, in sewing box with pair of pinking shears, quilting thimble and pattern instructions for quilted pillow or wall hanging. (Quilting thimble and instruction books available from Herrschners Quality Crafts).

SEAMSTRESS ▪ Packets of buttons and fancy trims, pin cushion, needle threader and attractive thimble, along with one or more catalogs for the home sewer.

STUDENT ▪ Packets of treats for those late-night study sessions, such as granola, dried fruit, nuts, carob bars. Add a jumbo bag of popcorn and electric hot-air popper.

TRAVELER ▪ Travel calculator (translates any currency to U.S. dollars); money belt/wallet, world alarm clock and security alarm all tucked into purse-size nylon tote bag to carry home gifts and souvenirs. All items available at The Travel Store.

10.

Wrapping It Up

Your gift may lie under the Christmas tree for days or even weeks before it is opened. During that time, the gift wrap you have used will be enjoyed by all if your package is wrapped with imagination.

Clever wrapping and packaging does not have to mean expensive paper and containers, however. Some of the most interesting won't cost you a penny.

Unusual Gift Wraps

1. Wrap a man's gift in outdated blueprint paper, or large sheet of graph paper.

2. Wrap an automotive theme gift such as a new key ring in a chamois cloth for his car.

3. Pack a crossword puzzle book and six sharpened pencils and a large eraser in a box. Wrap in crossword puzzle page of your city newspaper.

4. You can even use a green plastic trash sack for bulky gifts. Tie with huge bow of silver. Add color and pattern with plastic tape, if desired.

5. Use pages of the Wall Street Journal to wrap a gift for an executive.

6. Wrap a gift for a traveler in a map. Many are available free to members of auto associations.

7. Use your children's art work from school to wrap small gifts for relatives.

8. Buy end rolls of newsprint (available very inexpensively from your local newspaper) and spend an evening with your family drawing holiday or other designs. Its size and cost makes this a versatile yet far from costly wrapping paper.

9. At your local antique or second hand store you may be able to find very inexpensive (30 cents or less) sheet music, a great gift wrap for a gift for a musician.

10. Also available at second hand stores may be art prints you

wouldn't necessarily want for your walls, but which make very special gift wraps.

11. Dust jackets of old books you may be able to buy for under 50 cents at used book stores make fin gift wraps for small items, such as a new paperback book.

12. Wrap a hostess gift in squares of calico or geometric print you have bought at a sale of yard goods and trimmed with pinking shears. Tie with yarn, add stick of cinnamon or set of colorful plastic measuring spoons.

13. If your local stationery or trophy store has a stock of blue ribbons, use these as clever trims for your packages, which you have wrapped in white newsprint. Name of the person can be written in indigo ink on the package itself.

14. Coordinate gift and wrapping paper. For instance, a friend who collects antique fans would enjoy receiving an elegant fan of old lace wrapped in paper overprinted with fans. Remember, Christmas paper is not the only paper that can be used during the holidays.

15. Shop your import store for unusual designs in gift wrap paper. For a woman who collected statues of cows, a beautiful gift wrap paper featuring black and white cows on an emerald green background was found at such a store.

16. Use a colorful man's or woman's scarf to wrap a special gift.

17. Pages of a catalog that is outdated can also be used to wrap small gift items, or used to wrap an envelope containing a gift certificate for that store.

18. You can also use newspaper ads of department stores to gift wrap gift certificates from those shops.

19. That wine bottle you're taking as a hostess gift to a couple can be wrapped in aluminum foil from your kitchen. Tie it with a silver bow and add a sprig of mistletoe, or the newest wine bottle opener.

20. Shopping bags are highly decorative and have even become items of interest to collectors. They are great containers for that large gift item. Simply tape the top together and add scarlet holiday ribbon streamers and a gift tag.

21. You can even use plain brown paper as gift wrap. Add an elegant notary seal holding small ribbon streamers. Finish with gold elasticized tie and gold gift tag.

22. Large sheets of ledger paper used by accountants can be used to wrap gifts such as a pen and pencil set for a businesswoman.

23. Don't forget the pages of a holiday magazine, which can be used to wrap smaller items. An ad from Vogue, for instance, to wrap a set of earrings; a holiday food page to wrap a small cookery gift.

24. Large squares of felt make inexpensive gift wraps for special items.

25. Wrap a child's gift in the comic pages of the newspaper.

Interesting Gift Ties

You don't have to stick with the often expensive ribbon wraps and bows sold in stores. Try the following for unusual but decorative ties:

1. Buy skeins of yarn in holiday colors at your needlework shop.

2. Try wrapping gifts with satin hair ribbons from your variety store.

3. Buy a variety of items at a yardage store to tie packages. Try strips of calico material which you have cut with pinking shears, lengths of lace or strips of rick-rack and hemming tape.

4. Ordinary brown twine or string can make a striking package combined with brown paper trimmed with gold stars.

5. Tie a gift for a handyman with an extension cord.

6. Use a slender colorful scarf to tie up a gift for a woman or teen.

7. Drapery cording can be an unusual gift tie.

8. Inexpensive tinsel meant to decorate your tree can also tie up your packages.

9. Try wrapping a gift box of clothing with a belt in the recipient's size.

10. Tie one on with a tie! Use a gift necktie to wrap a box holding a man's shirt.

Clever Trims

1. Add a silver Christmas tree ornament to your package.

2. Gift for your husband? Do a Bacall, and tie a whistle to his package . . . if you want me, just whistle?

3. Use a recipe card for a tag. Add your own "recipe" for a happy holiday.

4. Tuck your five favorite microwavable recipes into a microwave-safe casserole for a friend who has a new microwave oven. Wrap in brown paper and trim with cut-outs of microwave ovens from catalogs or newspapers.

5. Buy a supply of gold notary seals and stick-on stars in many colors for attractive gift trims.

6. Do you have some artificial flowers that have outlived their usefulness? Use them to decorate a package.

7. Use seed packets to trim a gift for a gardener.

8. Dried herbs in small packets make great gift trims for a gift package for your favorite cook.

9. Use shoelaces to tie up a gift for a runner on your list.

10. Use a tape measure to wrap a gift for that dieter you're shopping for.

Try These Containers for Gifts

Apothecary jars, decorative tins from your local import store in a variety of sizes, refrigerator containers, empty stationery or candy boxes covered in calico or holiday wrap, apothecary jars, casserole dishes, mailing tubes, flower pots, empty jam jars (filled with an assortment of nuts or candy), small plastic cosmetic jars and bottles, tote bags, baskets in all sizes, candy dish, garden watering can, ashtray (large crystal ashtray can hold a new pipe and packets of tobacco), baking tins, teapot (fill with packets of gourmet tea), or inexpensive suitcase for a large, difficult-to-wrap gift.

Your kitchen is an inexhaustible supply of containers for both small and large gifts. Mixing bowls, cups and saucers, even that old chipped wine glass can hold interesting oddments such as plants, candy, holiday fruits or nuts, an array of cheeses, your own baked goods.

Don't neglect hardware stores, either, for unusual containers. Small tool boxes, fishing creels, and even a laundry basket for that extra large gift can all be found here.

When you are shopping, look at items in a different way, as possible containers for your Christmas gifts.

Reminder: Since not all gifts will be wrapped in non-traditional containers, do remember to collect gift boxes from department stores at which you shop during the year. Folded, they require little storage space, and are priceless when you suddenly have an array of gifts to wrap—and nothing to put them in!

Plan Your Gift Wrapping Supply Center Now

If you've ever had a dozen or more presents to wrap and have had to search for everything from tape to scissors and ribbon before you could begin, you will appreciate these tips.

Try setting up your gift center in an inexpensive used three-drawer chest you've purchased at a second hand store, or one of stiffened cardboard bought at the notions department of your favorite store.

However, anything will work. An old metal filing cabinet now relegated to the storage room, or even one or two large cardboard boxes will serve to make the task of Christmas wrapping easier for you.

What to Keep in Your Gift Center

In one drawer place a variety of wrapping paper for Christmas, including special wraps such as artwork done by your children, sheet music, art posters, etc. Add a supply of gift ribbons and bows to match, and white tissue paper suitable for lining holiday boxes and containers.

In this drawer you will also keep materials to aid in mailing packages. These will include parcel post labels, insulation materials to cushion contents of packages, pressure-sensitive filament or reinforced tape and paper for wrapping gifts to be mailed.

In the second drawer you will keep an assortment of gift wrap papers suitable for events such as showers, weddings, graduations, anniversaries, birthdays, Mother's Day and Father's Day. Add gift ribbon and bows in matching or contrasting colors.

In the last drawer, place scissors suitable for cutting paper, cellophane tape (two rolls), small gift enclosure cards, Christmas gift tags and seals, two pens and an assortment of birthday, anniversary and other cards. Add your Christmas cards to this drawer when they are purchased. Keep "Holiday Handbook" here for quick reference ideas.

On a closet shelf, keep a supply of boxes and other containers appropriate for holding gifts to be wrapped.

If you use these tips for wrapping your gifts and storing your gift supplies, your presents will not only be a memorable sight under that Christmas tree, but you will not have to spend precious time tracking down supplies you will need for gifts throughout the year.

The Mailing Solution

One of the most dreaded tasks for many of us at the holidays is wrapping gifts that must be mailed. First, the task always seems to come when we are most pressed for time, and second, we seem never to have the right supplies on hand.

One obvious solution is to have gifts wrapped for mailing at the department store where they were purchased. This is particularly helpful when such gifts were bought during the off-season, and no standing in long gift wrap lines was required.

However, if you must wrap and mail those gifts yourself, keeping mailing supplies in your gift center as suggested earlier, and using these tips from the United States Post Office will help make your job a little easier.

Packaging for Mailing

According to the U.S. Post Office, proper packaging and addressing of parcels is the best way to prevent damage and loss. Do use a container strong enough to protect the contents during handling.

Cushioning the contents to make sure they do not move within the container is also important for safe arrival. Some people find popcorn works well as an insulator; others buy special insulating material at their local stationer.

Do wrap each item enclosed individually, with enough padding to prevent damage. Separate wrapped items with padding or foamed plastic.

Do remember to place the name and address of the person to whom the package is addressed INSIDE the package as well as firmly affixed to the outside. Address should be printed and easily readable from two feet away.

After you have the parcel securely wrapped in sturdy paper (do not use gift wrap or tissue), wrap securely in pressure-sensitive filament or reinforced tape, being sure to reinforce the flaps and seams. Do not tie with twine or string; it could become entangled in post office processing machinery.

Be sure the address is legibly written on one side only. Do not use pencil, or any type of ink that is easily smeared. Be certain you have included a ZIP code, and that the package weight and size meets post office guidelines.

Packages mailed in the continental United States can weigh up to 70 pounds and measure up to 108 inches in length and girth combined. Remember that minimum sizes also apply on parcels processed by bulk mail center.

They must have a minimum length of six inches, width of at least three inches, height/thickness of at least one-fourth inch and weigh at least eight ounces.

Maximum standards for machinable parcels are 34 inches long, 17 inches in width and height and weigh 35 pounds. Maximum book weight is 25 pounds for such parcels.

The U.S. Post Office has two fine brochures on mailing parcels that you may find very helpful. Ask at your local post office branch for copies of Publication 2, "Packaging for Mailing," and Publication 227, "How to Prepare and Wrap Packages."

For faster delivery of your Yule packages, you might consider Priority Mail (two to three-day service); or Express Mail Service (overnight delivery). Of course, these are more expensive, but if it's essential that your package reach its destination by a certain date, definitely worth it!

The post office, however, is not the only means for sending packages to distant areas. United Parcel Service (UPS), Greyhound and Trailways bus lines also offer package delivery services worth checking into. You may be able to avoid long post office lines if you re mailing in December, and perhaps even ensure earlier delivery, by using such services.

However you plan to mail your packages this year, the best advice is to mail early—by mid or late November if at all possible.

After all, you can buy the most magnificent gift, but if it doesn't arrive by Christmas, the person to whom you send it may be disappointed indeed!

11.

Shopping By Mail

Confess! Weren't you hooked on buying by mail the first time you sent away as a child for a secret code ring, using a cereal boxtop?

The days seemed to drag until your package finally arrived. And then finally, it was here. You opened it slowly, to prolong the excitement, as your sister or brother looked on impatiently.

No shopping trip quite equals the excitement of awaiting a package we have ordered from a catalog. As adults, however, we have now discovered additional advantages to this armchair shopping.

Mail order firms offer career people an opportunity to shop at their leisure at home; for the elderly, no trips to town are necessary. Hobbyists can find the specialized items not available at their local stores, and handymen, sports enthusiasts, homemakers and students all enjoy browsing through catalogs.

The incredible variety of merchandise available offer us anything our heart desires, from elegant lingerie to the latest in camping equipment or bicycling gear.

However, as in any other shopping situation, the buyer must take some precautions. If you plan on shopping by mail this Christmas or next, do check carefully the Mail Order Shopping Tips that follow.

Although the author has presented the most current information available on each firm listed in this chapter, no endorsements or warranties as to the goods or the type of service provided by these listed firms is given. Hour Press and the author disclaim any liability for loss caused by errors or omissions.

This book is designed only as a guide to help you find products that are new, interesting, or of particular interest. It is up to you to shop as carefully through these catalogs as you would in the stores in your own hometown.

The mail order firms listed in this catalog are only a few of the thousands offering interesting products in the United States. There are many other catalogs space has not allowed us to list, and you will enjoy adding to your collection as you discover new firms that offer products by mail.

Mail Order Shopping Tips

1. If a firm has a toll-free line which may be used to request a catalog, use that rather than taking the extra time and expense necessary to request one by mail.

2. If you are making many catalog requests by mail, consider Xeroxing a form request letter. Be sure to enclose any fees requested. If you are enclosing coins, tape them to your request letter and write "Postmaster: Please Hand Cancel" on the outside of your envelope.

3. Keep a complete list of all catalogs you have requested, address, date requested, fees involved, and phone numbers, including toll-free information line. Note the date the catalog arrives. This can often give you an indication of how quickly the firm will also send your order. Use a separate page in your notebook for each catalog ordered.

4. Order early enough so that merchandise may be returned in case of damage, or dissatisfaction with the product. There is nothing worse than receiving a gift for someone special in mid-December, only to find it marred, broken or otherwise a disappointment. Never order less than five weeks before you want the merchandise.

5. Remember, you are protected by a Federal Trade Commission regulation which rules that the company must contact you about a delay over 30 days, and offer you a refund.

6. Be sure to read all fine print in your order form, including anticipated delivery date, and fill out required forms completely. Include all shipping and handling charges.

7. Never send cash. Use only money order, personal check, or your charge account.

8. If you plan to charge your purchases, be very certain the card you intend to use is honored at the mail order firm you plan to patronize. Many consumers feel uncomfortable sending their charge card number and expiration date by mail, but still others have done so and found the procedure both easy and practical.

9. Printing your name and address clearly is strongly advised, both on the order form itself and on the return envelope. If you have address labels, now is the time to use them.

10. In your Mail Order Notebook, keep a record of your order. This will include order date, your check number, name and address of the company, the item you ordered (including cost, color, size and number ordered), and the name and page number of the catalog in which the item is listed.

11. Be certain your order specifies when delivery is to be made to a third party, and whether this delivery is a gift. Note possible additional charge for third party delivery in catalog order instructions.

12. If you phone in an order and later confirm it in writing, be sure you state clearly on the written order that it is merely a phone order confirmation. If you don't, you may find yourself being billed for two identical orders.

13. If you haven't received your order within one week of the time promised, and time is critical, phone the firm at the number listed in your mail order notebook and check with the order department.

14. Open and inspect the items ordered immediately after delivery. If goods are damaged or you are disappointed in the quality of the items ordered, return them promptly with a brief letter stating your reasons and requesting your money back, a credit on your charge account, or other merchandise of equal value.

15. In your notebook, write a brief comment on your impression of goods received, any damage noted, and whether or not you would be willing to order from that firm again.

16. Deal only with firms that offer money back guarantees, or otherwise guarantee satisfaction to their customers. Most offer a 30-day period for exchange, refund or credit transactions.

Shopping By Mail is Half the Fun

Even if you don't have time this year to order your gifts by mail, send for these catalogs now. You will enjoy looking at them during the quieter days of January, and perhaps enjoy sending for items for birthday, shower or anniversary gifts.

Among the most popular mail order catalogs are:

BLOOMINGDALE'S
Salem, VA 24156
Catalog: $3 (request ready-to-wear catalog)
Catalog: $4 (request home furnishings and housewares catalog)
"Bloomie's" has long been a New York favorite. Now you, too, can shop from the comfort of your armchair.

BROOKS BROTHERS
346 Madison Ave., New York, NY 10017
Catalog: Free
Few of us haven't heard of this fine clothing store for men.

GUMP'S
P.O. Box 7301, San Francisco, CA 94120
Catalog: $3 (series of four books)
San Francisco residents love this historic firm tucked into Union Square. They do much of their shopping for crystal, china, stationery, and other gifts here.

MARSHALL FIELD
Box 1165, Chicago, IL 60690
Catalog: $2
Chicago residents feel about Marshall Field's the way New York natives feel about Bloomingdale's. General merchandise is available here.

NEIMAN-MARCUS
P.O. Box 2968, Dallas, TX 75221
Catalog: $5
Who hasn't pined over the beautifully displayed gifts in this Christmas catalog?

Specialty catalogs include:

Art and Books
ABRACADADA
P.O. Box 210367, San Francisco, CA 94121
Catalog: Free
Rubber stamps are "in" these days, and this Bay Area firm has stamps featuring everything from acrobats and clowns to Tina Turner, Prince, cars and op-art.

ART INSTITUTE OF CHICAGO
Michigan Ave. at Adams St., Chicago, IL 60603
Catalog: $1
This full color gift catalog features outstanding art reproductions, Christmas cards, calendars, stationery, scarves, ties and jewelry.

ART POSTER CO.
Ste. 234, 29555 Northwestern Hwy., Southfield, MI 48034
Catalog: $2
Art prints and posters.

BARNES & NOBLE BOOKSTORES, INC.
126 Fifth Ave., New York, NY 10011-5666
Catalog: Free
Booksellers since 1873, this firm has more than books. Items include a lighted globe of the world, a device for embossing stationery, and tape cassette holders.

BOOKLOOK
5122 Maple Ave., Warwick, NY 10990
Catalog: $1
For the booklover who yearns for an out-of-print book. List title(s) desired.

CHARRETTE
31 Olympia Ave., Woburn, MA 01888
Catalog: $3.50 (294 pages)
Any architect, artist or engineer on your holiday list would be delighted to find this catalog under the holiday tree.

DICK BLICK COMPANY
P.O. Box 521, Henderson, NV 89015
Catalog: $3.50 (370 pages—worth every penny!)
Comprehensive catalog offers an incredible array of supplies for artists and educators. Nice gift in itself for an artist friend.

FREER GALLERY OF ART
Smithsonian Institution, 12th St. at Jefferson Dr. SW, Washington, DC 20560
Catalog: Free
You will find reproductions of paintings and other artifacts offered in this interesting 72-page catalog.

HERO ARTS RUBBER STAMPS
P.O. Box 5234, Berkeley, CA 94705
Catalog: Free
This firm has a line of rubber stamps especially made to upgrade young students. Many teachers now use rubber stamps as teaching aids.

METROPOLITAN MUSEUM OF ART
255 Gracie Station, New York, NY 10028
Catalog: $1
More than 100 pages here of unusual gifts, reproduced from works of art in this great museum's collections. Priced from less than $5 to more than $500.

MISTER FRAME
P.O. Box 683, Manassas, VA 22110
Catalog: $1
Have art you'd like to frame as a gift? Send for this catalog that features supplies for the "framer."

NERVO INTERNATIONAL
4365 Arnold Ave., Naples, FL 33942
Catalog: $3
Supplies for the stained glass artist.

PEERLESS RATTAN
P.O. Box 636, Yonkers, NY 10701
Catalog: 25 cents
Lists supplies for those interested in basketry, caning and rush work.

SCULPTURE ASSOCIATES
40 E. 19th St., New York, NY 10003
Catalog: $2
Know a friend who's interested in sculpting? This catalog will give you dozens of ideas.

SELMAN, L.H. LTD.
761 Chestnut St., Santa Cruz, CA 95060
Catalog: $10
Pricey, but full-color catalog of elegant paperweights is terrific if you're a collector!

SMITHSONIAN INSTITUTION
P.O. Box 199, Washington, DC 20560
Request free Smithsonian catalogue
Great gifts here for everyone!

Clothing (Children)
BRIGHT'S CREEK
Bay Point Place, Hampton, VA 23653
Catalog: Free
Children's wear from newborn to 12 years of age.

HANNA ANDERSSON
422 NW Eighth Ave., Portland, OR 97209
Swedish quality in 100 percent cotton clothing for your children, from receiving blankets and baby shirts to tights, dresses and sweaters for the older set.

Clothing (Men)
A. SULKA AND COMPANY
711 Fifth Ave., New York, NY 10022
Catalog: $2
It's just fun to browse through this pictorial collection of men's classic clothing and haberdashery.

CABLE CAR CLOTHIERS
150 Post St., San Francisco, CA 94108
Try a one-year subscription for $3
Men's clothing and accessories in an exciting array from this noted San Francisco firm.

KING SIZE COMPANY
24 Forest St., Brockton, MA 02402
Free 96-page catalog
Clothing for the larger man. Catalog includes shoes and accessories.

Clothing (Women)
AVON FASHIONS
Avon Lane, Newport News, VA 23630
Free catalog
This firm prides itself on its selection of fine quality merchandise, supervised at every stage of construction. From career-oriented dresses to weekend wear, lingerie, shoes and accessories, Avon Fashions has it. Unconditional guarantee offered.

CAREER GUILD
6412 Vapor Lane, Niles, IL 60648
Free catalog (32 pages)
Interested in coordinated career fashions? This firm features quality clothing for working women.

GARNET HILL
P.O. Box 262, Franconia, NH 03580
Free catalog
Natural fiber clothing for everyone, plus other natural fiber home products.

L.L. BEAN
2251 Casco St., Freeport, ME 04033
Free catalog
Features active and casual wear for women and men who enjoy the outdoors. Great gift ideas, all fully guaranteed. A classic!

Women's Larger Sizes
FASHION CATALOG
2300 Southeastern Ave., Indianapolis, IN 46207
Free catalog
If you wear a larger size, you don't have to compromise on clothing anymore that just isn't "you." Sizes range from 34 to 52, shoe sizes to EEE width. Real fashion choices here at moderate prices.

LERNER WOMAN
Lerner Plaza, Acton, IN 46258
Free one-year subscription
Everything from lingerie to sportswear and pantyhose for the larger woman. Wide array of sizes in clothing and shoes.

SPIEGEL, INC.
P.O. Box 7623, Chicago, IL 60680
Free catalog
Request "Large-Size Women's Apparel catalog." Other Speigel offerings include Fashions and Accessories, Petites, Women's Designer Fashions and Career Wear.

Intimate Apparel
FREDERICK'S OF HOLLYWOOD
6610 Hollywood Blvd., Hollywood, CA 90028
Eleven-issue subscription, $3
Who hasn't heard of this mail order firm specializing in seductive lingerie and clothing? Fun!

INTIMIQUE
40 Winterbrook Way, Meredith, NJ 03253
Free catalog
Intimate apparel for women.

SWANN SELECTIONS
400 National Blvd., Lexington, NC 27292
Free catalog
Designer sleepwear, lingerie, hosiery and leisure wear.

VICTORIA'S SECRET
P.O. Box 16590, Columbus, OH 43216
Catalog: $3 (one year subscription)
Designer lingerie offered is elegant and sensuous.

Maternity Wear
FIFTH AVENUE MATERNITY
P.O. Box 21826, Seattle, WA 98111
Catalog: $2
This firm specializes in fashionable maternity clothing of fine quality.

MOTHERS WORK
P.O. Box 40121, Philadelphia, PA 19106
Catalog, $3 (refundable with first order)
Enjoy browsing through their fine collection of maternity business suits and dresses, complete with swatches and fit guide.

RE CREATIONS
P.O. Box 091038, Columbus, OH 43209
Catalog: $2
Fashions fit sizes 4 to 14, and make it easy and affordable to look your best while maintaining your professional image.

Collectibles/Hobbies
BEAR-IN-MIND
20 Beharrell St., West Concord, MA 01742
Catalog: Free
What a joy for those who have loved teddy bears since childhood! Give a gift certificate (order by phone, 617-369-1167), which is accompanied by catalog.

THE BEAR NECESSITIES
72 Broad St., Boston, MA 02110
Catalog: Free
What bear collector can ever have enough catalogs about their favorite collectible! This is another great catalog for that bear bobbyist on your list.

H.L. CHILDS AND SONS
P.O. Box 355, Northampton, MA 01060
Catalog: $1.50
Do you have a collector of miniatures on your holiday list? Here's a great source of gifts, or simply a catalog to tuck in a Christmas stocking.

COLLECTORS' GUILD, INC.
1625 Bathgate Ave., Bronx, NY 10457-8101
Catalog: Free
Calendars, jewelry and collector's prints abound in this 46-page catalog.

CURRENT
Express Processing Cntr., Colorado Springs, CO 80941
Catalog: Free
You can spend a delightful afternoon browsing through their Christmas catalog, chock full of Christmas gifts and cards, wrapping paper and other holiday goodies!

FALKS
P.O. Box 128, New Richmond, OH 45157
Everything from personalized car mats and solid silver money clips to game and travel accessories. Great ideas for gifts for the men on your list.

H.E. HARRIS AND COMPANY
645 Summer St., Boston, MA 02210
Catalog, $3.75 (over 300 pages)
What an exciting gift for a stamp collector! This hefty catalog lists an incredible array of stamp collecting supplies, stamps and stamp albums.

POTPOURRI
204 Worcester St., Wellesley, MA 02181
Handcrafted collectible dolls, plus a true potpourri of everything from personalized welcome mats and wall hangings to Christmas decorations.

INTERNATIONAL COINS AND CURRENCY
P.O. Box 218, Montpelier, VT 05602
Free catalog (18 pages)
Rare coins for the coin collector fill these pages.

KRUCKEMEYER AND COHN (Est. 1895)
309-11 Main St., Evansville, IN 47708
Catalog: Free
This firm is the source of those very collectible David Winter English cottages. You'll find the complete collection, including a wonderful fairy tale castle. Free shipping.

LAS VEGAS GOLF AND TENNIS
4813 Paradise Road, Las Vegas, NV 89109-7153
Catalog: $2
Do you have a golfer on your Christmas list? What better gift than an item from this catalog, which is brimful of great gifts for golfers and tennis players.

LIBERTY GIFTS
2324 Liberty St., Trenton, NJ 08629
Catalog, $3
Know someone who collects Hummel porcelain figurines? Why not give this catalog as a gift, or order a figurine you know your friend hasn't yet acquired?

OFFICIAL NBA CATALOG
Unique Merchandise Mart, Bldg. #73, Hanover, PA 17333
Collectibles from your favorite NBA teams for that man in your life.

STANDARD DOLL CO.
2383 31st St., Long Island City, NY 11105
Catalog, $3
A catalog for the doll hobbyist. You'll find dollmaking accessories, repair supplies, sewing notions and many other items necessary for that doll collector on your list.

TCMA LTD.
220 12th Ave., New York, NY 10001
Catalog: Free
If your husband, brother or son is a baseball fan, they're bound to enjoy a gift from this catalog.

Crystal, China and Silver

REJECT CHINA SHOPS

34 Beauchamp Pl., Knightsbridge, London SW3, England

Free catalog (Be sure to include enough postage on your catalog request!)

English fine bone china, earthenware and crystal from leading manufacturers is featured in this mail order catalog. "For first quality rejects, you can't beat our prices" this firm insists. "We have enormous savings over U.S. retail prices even when all postal and insurance charges have been included."

REPLACEMENTS, LTD.

1510 Holbrook, Greensboro, NC 27403

If you have a friend who is constantly bemoaning the fact that she cannot find any pieces in her discontinued china or crystal pattern, try writing this firm for information or call them at 919-275-7224.

SPOON WORLD INTERNATIONAL

P.O. Box 1215, Bellingham, WA 98227

Free brochure

You'll find the perfect gift for the spoon collector on your list. Free brochure lists spoons by state, country, city and for Christmas, Mother's Day, Easter, Zodiac, even Halley's Comet or the Statue of Liberty.

TIFFANY & CO.

727 Fifth Ave., New York, NY 10022

Catalog: $3

This is definitely a catalog that's worth your $3 investment, just for the pleasure of looking at more than 200 pages of fine crystal and china, jewelry and silver.

WALTER DRAKE SILVER EXCHANGE

5039 Drake Bldg., Colorado Springs, Co 80940

Free flatware pattern identification directory

This firm offers a sterling and silverplate pattern matching service. It carries more than 2,000 patterns in stock. Send pattern name and manufacturer and request free price list.

Food and Nutrition

CALLAWAY GARDENS COUNTRY STORE
Pine Mountain, GA 31822
Free catalog
You don't have to travel to this delightful Southern resort to enjoy homestyle foods like smoked ham and bacon.

CHEESE OF ALL NATIONS (Est. 1935)
153 Chambers St., New York, NY 10007
Catalog: $1
Phone: (212) 732-0752 Gift certificates
This firm is a direct importer from individual cheesemakers throughout the world. Many cheeses are made especially for them. They guarantee fast delivery in any quantity.

CHARLES LOEB (Mr. Spiceman)
615 Palmer Rd., Yonkers, NY 10701
Catalog: Free   Gift certificates over $10
Gourmet housewares, accessories, teas, gifts are all available at this firm. Most of all, however, do consider buying your fresh spices in bulk at considerable savings.

CHINESE KITCHEN
P.O. Box 218, Stirling, NJ 07980
(201) 665-2234 (Phone number is for orders only)
Catalog: $1 ($2 refund coupon with first order)
"Your mail order Oriental grocery store" lives up to its billing. Everything from cookbooks and a beginner's kit for those cooking Chinese for the first time, to utensils, dinnerware, Chinese teas, sauces and condiments. Invaluable if you love Chinese food!

COLLIN STREET BAKERY
Box 1032, Corsicana, TX 75110
This firm has been producing juicy holiday fruitcakes filled with pecans and fruit since 1896. They guarantee delivery in two weeks and enclose a gift card. Call them at 800-624-5041 to order.

DAKIN FARM
Route 7, Ferrisburg, VT 05456
Catalog: Free (16 pages, color)
Smoked Vermont ham and bacon, pure maple syrup and cheddar cheese from this Northeastern firm.

DEAN & DELUCA
110 Greene St., Suite 304, New York, NY 10012
Catalog: Free
The best in international food, from dried porcini Italian mushrooms to Tuscan rusks from La Tempesta.

DELICACIES NORTHWEST
531 SW Macadam, Suite 218, Portland, OR 97201
Catalog: Free (16 pages, color)
Food gift baskets heaped with foods from the Northwest.

GOODBEE PECAN PLANTATIONS
P.O. Box 3890, Albany, GA 31706
Catalog: Free
Love pecan pie or pecan bars? Order these special South Georgia pecans for a taste treat. Give some to friends, use the rest in your holiday baking.

GREEN MOUNTAIN SUGAR HOUSE
Ludlow, VT 05149
Catalog: Free
Gourmet items from this Vermont firm, including maple products and cheese.

HARRY AND DAVID
Bear Creek Orchards, Medford, OR 97501
Free brochure
(To order, call 800-547-3033)
Noted for their Fruit-of-the-Month club offerings, which begin in January with crisp mountain apples. Other delectable monthly fruits might include royal oranges, kiwi berries, peaches, pears, nectarines and pineapples. Prices begin at under $50.

JAFFEE BROS. (Est. 1948)
P.O. Box 636, Valley Center, CA 92082
Catalog: Free
National distributors of natural foods. Try their nuts, grain, pasta, seeds, unsalted nut butters, beans, carob confections, jams and cooking oil. Send someone you love a special gift package.

MAISON GLASS, INC.
52 E. 58th St., New York, NY 10022
Catalog: Free (minimum order, $15)
You'd better eat before you look at this catalogue of international delicacies, or you'll want to order everything! If it's a gourmet treat, Maison Glass will have it. You can put on the dinner of your dreams for 12 at an elegant Manhattan townhouse ($12,000), or enjoy bittersweet chocolate wafer thins from Switzerland for less than $6. It's all here from caviar and cheesecake to quail eggs and truffle soup. Give the catalog to your favorite gourmet cook.

SELECT ORIGINS
Box N, Southampton, NY 11968
Catalog: Free
Find quality herbs, spices, oil, vinegar, pasta, tea and coffee in this special catalog that would make a fine stocking stuffer for a friend who enjoys fine cookery.

SIR THOMAS LIPTON'S TRADING COMPANY
Mail Order Division, P.O. Box 2005, Nashua, NH 03061
Free brochure (6 pages)
Order toll-free (800-932-0488)
Tea-loving friend? Send her a membership in the tea-of-the month club, or an individual canister of rare premium tea such as Nuwar Eliya from Sri Lanka, Yunnan from Yunnan Province in China, or Orange Gardens Herbal Tea. Prices include shipping and handling.

THANKSGIVING COFFEE COMPANY
Box 1918, Fort Bragg, CA 95437 (707) 964-4711
Free brochure and mail order information
Throughout California's Wine Country, restaurants, inns and hotels pamper their guests with this fine coffee.

E.M. TODD CO., INC. (Est. 1779)
P.O. Box 5167, Richmond, VA 23220
Toll-free telephone orders, 800-368-5026.
Catalog: Free
This firm has been in business for two centuries, with customers savoring the distinct character and flavors of their Virginia hams and bacon. Allows enclosure of personal gift card.

VERMONT COUNTRY STORE (Est. 1946)
P.O. Box 3000, Manchester Center, VT 05255-3000
Catalog: Free (96 pages)
Stoneground cereals and flours, cheese and maple products, housewares and a delightful array of "penny" candy here.

WALNUT ACRES (Est. 1946)
Penns Creek, PA 17862
24-hour order line, (1-717-837-0601)
Catalog: Free
This 40-page color catalog featuring organically raised natural foods is a pleasure to peruse. You can find foods direct from the farm (500 acres of chemical-free soil), recipes, granolas, seeds and grains, natural extracts, dried fruits, raw shelled nuts, fruitcake, seasonings and organic herbs. Anyone on your Christmas list interested in health and nutrition would welcome this catalog, or some special item in it.

Gardening
BLUESTONE
7205 Middle Ridge, Madison, OH 44057
Catalog: Free
This firm offers the finest plants in more than 300 varieties.

BRECK'S (Est. 1818)
Mail Order Center, P.O. Box 1757, Peoria, IL 61656
Catalog: Free
This firm has served American gardeners from Holland since 1818. Jewel-tone hyacinths, apricot tulips, giant daffodils, colorful Dutch iris—all are available in this full-color catalog.

CAPRILAND'S HERB FARM
Silver Street, Coventry, CT 06238
Catalog: Free
You can buy more than an incredible array of herbs at this firm, including fragrances, potpourri, essential oils, pomander balls, calendars, napkins, bookmarks and herb teas.

GREENWOOD NURSERY
2 El Camino Real, Goleta, CA 93117
Catalog: $1
Selections of new and classic varieties of that perennial gardener's favorite, daylilies.

ROSEHILL FARM
Box 406, Galena, MD 21635
Catalog: Free
This catalog features an extensive array of beautiful, hardy miniature roses that can be grown either indoors or out.

SUCCULENTS
12712 Stockton Blvd., Galt, CA 95632
Catalog: $2
If you have a friend who specializes in raising these interesting plants, tuck this catalog in her Christmas stocking.

Gifts
ADAM YORK
Unique Merchandise Mart, Bldg. 6, Hanover, PA 17333
Catalog: $2
This firm digs deep for items that offer you unique differences, the kind of gifts, clothing and other products not easily found elsewhere. In addition there is tollfree shopping, immediate shipping and full guarantee.

HAMMACHER SCHLEMMER
11013 Kenwood Road, Cincinnati, OH 45242-1815
Catalog: Free
This firm's catalog has one of the most unique collections of gifts anywhere. You can find everything from an indoor putting green to a talking computer bridge player. Many gifts for the traveler and athlete here, as well as hobbyists, executives and gardeners.

JEWISH MUSEUM SHOP
1109 Fifth Ave., New York, NY 10028
Catalog: Free
Give a Jewish friend this catalog of gifts from the museum. She'll be delighted!

METROPOLITAN MUSEUM OF ART
255 Gracie Station, New York, NY 10028
Catalog: $1
Their holiday catalog is a Christmas tradition. You'll find everything from cards and prints to reproductions and other special art-related gifts. Don't miss it.

MILES KIMBALL
251 Bond St., Oshkosh, WI 54906-0002
Catalog: Free
This full color catalog presents hundreds of gifts and gadgets, personalized products, holiday decorations, housewares, gadgets and toys, many under $5.

SAN FRANCISCO MUSEUM OF MODERN ART
Museum Books Mail Order, Van Ness Ave. at McAllister St., San Francisco, Ca 94102
Catalog: $1 (32 pages)
You'll find lots of Christmas ideas including cards, books, games and calendars in this traditional holiday catalog.

SHANNON MAIL ORDER CGI
Shannon Duty-Free Airport, Ireland
Catalog: $1 (Remember to put enough postage on your catalogue request!)
Maybe you can't go to Ireland this year, but you can enjoy this 60-page catalog with gifts from Europe at affordable prices.

SHARPER IMAGE
680 Davis St., San Francisco, CA 94111
Catalog: Free
What fun it is to read this catalog! You'll find everything from a Sound Soother which uses white noise resembling surf, rainfall or waterfall; to a Guardian Angel, a transmitter that clips to your child's belt, an affordable electronic system that monitors your child's activities, letting you know if he has wandered out of the safety range.

SPENCER GIFTS
480 Spencer Bldg., Atlantic City, NJ 08411
Free catalog
Over 100 pages of homey gifts here. From decorator spoon rack and automatic card shuffler to a child's name puzzle custom carved in wood, you'll enjoy taking a look at the unusual gifts.

TRIFLES
P.O. Box 819075, Dallas, TX 75381-9075
Catalog: $3
Everything from the practical to the outrageous you'll find in this holiday gift catalog. Catalog fee entitles you to a full year of Trifles mailings.

WHOLE EARTH ACCESS (Est. 1969)
2950 Seventh St., Berkeley, CA 94710
Catalog: $3
Californians love this firm, a veritable general store carrying everything from clothing and appliances to chain saws and rototillers, all at sizeable discounts.

Home Decorating
ABERCROMBIE & FITCH (Est. 1892)
P.O. Box 70858, Houston, TX 77270-0858
Christmas Catalog: Free
This famed firm has a wonderful holiday catalog where you will find not only home accessories, but creative gifts for everyone on your list. Don't miss it!

CAROL WRIGHT GIFTS
3601 NW 15th Street, Lincoln, NE 68544
Catalog: Free
Wide array of gift items for the home.

DOMESTICATIONS
Unique Merchandise Mart, # 40, Hanover, PA 17333-0040
Catalog: Free
Wonderful bed linen and other household items here, from zebra-striped sheets to a teddy bear comforter set.

HANOVER HOUSE
Unique Merchandise Mart., Bldg. 2, Hanover, PA 17333
Catalog: $1
From rainbow bright vinyl paper clips to microwave potato rings and leg wallet holders, this catalog has it. Special pages with gifts under $1.

HARRIET CARTER
Dept. 36HH, North Wales, PA 19455
Catalog: Free
Everything from holiday decorations to Garfield pillows.

HOLST, INC.
1118 West Lake, Box 370, Tawas City, MI 48763
Catalog: Free
You'll enjoy the assortment of gifts in this one! Weathervanes, windmills, bird feeders, even famous railroad emblems.

LILLIAN VERNON
610 S. Fulton Ave., Mount Veron, NY 10550
Catalog: Free
Over 100 pages of exciting gifts for everyone on your list, plus holiday decora-tions galore in this fun Christmas catalog.

WILDWOOD GALLERY, INC.
P.O. Box 300, Syracuse, NY 13205-0300
Hundreds of unique and affordable decorative accessories, with complete cus-tomer satisfaction guaranteed. From antique fire engine and train wall plaques to wicker, brass and wood accessories, you'll find lots to enjoy here.

Kitchenware/Cookware
THE CHEF'S CATALOG
3915 Commercial Ave., Northbrook, IL 60062
Catalog: $2 (one-year subscription)
Great gifts for cooking and entertaining in this well-known firm's catalog.

S.E. RYKOFF & CO.
Market Street Station, P.O. Box 21467, Los Angeles, CA 90021
Catalog: Free
Commercial quality cookware in this interesting catalog.

WILLIAMS-SONOMA
Mail Order Dept., P.O. Box 7456, San Francisco, CA 94120-7456
Catalog: Free
This firm has been serving serious cooks since 1956, and offers a large catalog filled with colorful illustrations of kitchen equipment ranging from paella pans to simmer pots, French bread pans to copper confiture pans. Any cook on your list would enjoy a gift from this catalog.

WORLD'S FARE
P.O. Box 5678, Smithtown, NY 11787
Catalog: $1
You'll find international cooking equipment and accessories at this New York firm.

Miscellaneous

AMERICA'S HOBBY CENTER, INC.
146 W. 22nd St., New York, NY 10011-2466
Catalog: Free
Someone on your gift list who loves model railroad systems? Tuck this catalog in his stocking!

CASWELL-MASSEY
111 Eighth Ave., New York, NY 10011
Catalog: Free
Who wouldn't enjoy looking at a catalog from this long-established firm? You'll find toiletries, cosmetics, personal care items and luxury bath products.

CHILDREN'S BOOK AND MUSIC CENTER
P.O. Box 1130, Santa Monica, CA 90406-1130
Catalog: Free
What a great catalog for parents who want to provide enrichment material for their chldren.

DEFENDER INDUSTRIES, INC. (Est. 1938)
P.O. Box 820, New Rochelle, NY 10802-0820
Catalog: Free (over 200 pages)
This marine buyer guide promises "the largest inventory at the best values anywhere in the U.S." Great for the boating enthusiast.

EDDIE BAUER
P.O. Box 3700, Seattle, WA 98130-0006
Nearly 100 pages of exciting merchandise from this firm, including wonderful goose down products, and great outdoor clothing such as parkas, hunting vests and fairisle sweaters. Satisfaction guaranteed.

FAO SCHWARZ
745 Fifth Ave., New York, NY 10151
Catalog: Free
This great New York toy store is known all over the world!

FLEUR DE SANTE
P.O. Box 16090, Fort Lauderdale, FL 33318
Catalog: Free
This firm offers herbal beauty care "from Scandinavia to you."

HANOVER HOUSE
Unique Merchandise Mart, Bldg. 2, Hanover, PA 17333
Catalog: Free
This color catalog features items from pocket siren lights and hideaway wall safes to a super salad slicer.

THE HORCHOW COLLECTION
P.O. Box 819066, Dallas, TX 75381-9066
This great Texas firm has thrilled residents with its wonderful Christmas catalog for years. Items for the home, jewelry, apparel, decorative accessories.

LAURA ASHLEY BY POST
1300 MacArthur Blvd., Mahwah, NJ 07430 (1-800-223-6917)
If you've ever admired Laura Ashley items, here's a chance to browse through pages of fashions in her inimitable style. Allow 14 days for delivery.

LEANIN' TREE
Box 9500, Boulder, CO 80301
Catalog: Free
Great assortment of Christmas cards. Includes themes such as Western, ski, train and wildlife.

MARKLINE
P.O. Box C, Belmont, MA 02178
Catalog: Free
From oscillating fans to movie-to-video transfer system, this firm has it.

MISCO
One Misco Plaza, Holmdel, NJ 07733
Catalog: Free
Computer supplies and accessories for that computer buff on your list.

NAT SHERMAN
711 Fifth Ave., New York, NY 10022
Catalog: Free
For smoker's accessories, cigars, a wide array of cigarettes, pipe tobacco, as well as other items for the smoker, this catalog can't be beat.

J.C. WHITNEY & CO.
P.O. Box 8410, Chicago, IL 60680
Catalog: Free
This huge (nearly 300 pages) catalog is a gift in itself for the automotive buff. You'll find everything from wrenches to block assemblies between its covers.

Needlework/Crafts

CRAFT BASKET
Colchester, CT 06415
Catalog: Free one year subscription
Creative craft kits, including quilting supplies, needlework items and frames. Order shipped within 24 hours.

CROSS CREEK
4114 Lakeside Drive, Richmond, CA 94806
Catalog: $1
Over 1,000 designs. Packed with fascinating counted cross stitch samplers, frames, designs, metal punch designs, samplers and many more items to warm the heart of the ardent needleworker.

CROSS STITCH & COUNTRY CRAFTS
Subscription: Six issues, $14.97
This magazine for cross stitchers and those who enjoy creating country crafts is published six times a year. Buy a subscription for yourself, get one for a needleworking friend for only $9.97. Sample issue? Send $2.95.

HEARTHSIDE QUILTS
P.O. Box 429, Shelburne, VT 05482
Catalog: $2
Top quality quilt kits featured. Try your hand at placemats, pillows, wall hangings and country quilts graded from beginner to expert. Includes fabric swatches and discount coupons.

HERRSCHNER'S
Hoover Road, Stevens Point, WI 54481
Catalog: Free
This 72-page catalog has items that would delight any seamstress on your list.

LACIS
2982 Adeline St., Berkeley, CA 94703
Catalog: $1
This textile arts center specializes in antique laces, textiles, antique needlework and one-of-a-kind textile pieces. You will also find equipment and services geared to the lesser known textile crafts, plus antique needlework tools and findings.

LOVE AND MONEY CRAFTS
P.O. Box 987, Ann Arbor, MI 48106
Catalog: $1 (one-year subscription)
Lap weaving and country craft kits, loom and needlework accessories, as well as Christmas items here.

THE STITCHERY
204 Worcester Turnpike, Wellsley Hills, MA 02181
Catalog: Free
Needlecrafts and kits for the beginning and experienced hobbyist.

WOOL DESIGN LATCH HOOK KITS
8916 York Rd., Charlotte, NC 28210
Catalog: Free
Quality needlepoint and latch hook kits.

Pets
ANIMAL CITY (Est. 1965)
P.O. Box 1076, La Mesa, CA 92041-0318
Catalog: Free
Why pay retail prices at expensive stores when you can buy essential pet supplies here? Everything from novelties and grooming equipment to cages and bird and aquarium supplies available.

HARRIET CARTER
Dept. 36, North Wales, PA 19455
Catalog: Free
Although this is a fascinating catalog with general items, you will also find interesting pet-related items such as a book on "Cathletics," which shows you how to exercise and amuse your favorite feline.

AUDUBON WORKSHOP
1501 Paddock Dr., Northbrook, IL 60062
Catalog: Free
Any birdwatcher on your list would enjoy this catalog that features an array of items including feeders.

MASTER GEORGE, INC.
Rt. 1, Box 85, California, KY 41007
Catalog: Free
Dogs should be remembered at the holidays, too. You'll have fun choosing gifts that are unique and personalized for the family dog.

PEDIGREES, THE PET CATALOG
15 Turner Dr., Spencerport, NY 14559
Catalog: Free
Owning your pet will be a little easier with supplies from this firm.

UNITED PHARMACAL CO., INC.
P.O. BOX 969, St. Joseph, MO 64502
Catalog: Free (112 pages)
You don't have to be a veterinarian to order from this complete line of dog, cat and horse supplies at wholesale prices.

VERMONT COUNTRY STORE (See listing under Food)
Order a pet bed filled with natural cedar shavings, with an aroma that repels fleas and ticks (under $30 for dogs, under $20 for cats).

Travel
BANANA REPUBLIC TRAVEL AND SAFARI CLOTHING CO.
P.O. Box 7347, San Francisco, CA 94120
Catalog: $1 (Order catalog items toll-free 800-527-5200)
This well-known firm offers items such as 100-percent cotton Bombay shirts (under $20), or all-cotton bush vests (under $40)—garments that are difficult to find anywhere else.

BOOK PASSAGE
51 Tamal Vista Blvd., Corte Madera, CA 94925
Catalog: Free
Request their travel books, guides and maps catalog. You'll find great reading and all the information you need to travel anywhere in the world.

CAMPMOR
P.O. Box 999, Paramus, NJ 07653-0999 (1-800-526-4784)
Catalog: Free
If you're traveling and have a dental emergency far from help, what can you do? Campmor has the answer with its dental emergency kit that can handle everything from a lost filling to a lost tooth (under $10). There are many other helpful products in this catalog, from cold compresses to emergency drinking water tablets.

GOLDEN AGE TRAVELLERS
1520 Union St., San Francisco, CA 94123
(Inside California, call 800-652-2361; in San Francisco,
call 415-563-2361; other areas, call 800-258-8880)
Free cruise catalog
If there's a senior adult on your shopping list, why not surprise him or her with a membership in Golden Age Travellers? Inexpensive membership is worth it alone in providing free home pick-up service to its members on cruises and tours.

EAGLE CREEK TRAVEL GEAR
P.O. Box 744, Solana Beach, CA 92075
Catalog: Free   Phone: (619) 755-9399
For those who must travel with a baby, this firm makes a special diaper pack knapsack with zip-down changing pad. Many pockets for easy storage. Also stocks many other travel items. Send for their free catalog.

HOFFRITZ
515 West 24th Street, New York, NY 10011
Catalog: Free
Travelers may be interested in the mini travel Water-Pik from this firm, as well as other items for the globe-trotter.

INDIANA CAMP SUPPLY, INC.
P.O. Box 211, Hobart, IN 46342
Catalog: Free   Phone: (219) 947-2525
Buy a tough thermometer which measures outside temperature when you're outdoors and has a wind chill chart on the back. If you're hiking, try the digital pedometer, a device to measure distance walked that clips to your belt. These are only two of the many items featured for campers.

REI
1338 San Pablo Ave., Berkeley, CA 94720
Catalog: Free   Phone: (415) 527-4140
How about a water purifier which can filter out herbicides, pesticides, asbestos and many other chemicals for your favorite camper?

TRAVEL STORE
56 1/2 North Santa Cruz Ave., Los Gatos, CA 95030
Catalog: Free   Phone: (408) 354-9909
This California firm offers travel books and guides, maps, passport and visa photos, and products that range from adaptor plugs and collapsible cups to inflatable hangers, medical travel cases and metric converters. Gift certificates, free "Tips for the Traveler" booklet, free bookmarks and how-to-pack tips, as well as free brochure on foreign electrical requirements.

Wine
WINDSOR VINEYARDS, P.O. Box 368, Windsor, CA 95492
Free catalog
This California winery puts out a 20-page catalog filled with gifts of fine wine from famed Sonoma County wine country.

WINE AMBIANCE, Box J, Rolling Hills Estates, CA 90274
Catalog: $2
Have a wine enthusiast on your list? Check this 32-page catalog for accessories and gifts to please his heart!

12.

Your Holiday Party

If you are planning to have a party during the Christmas season, here are some guidelines that will help you create a holiday happening people will long remember—and one you will look back on as the easiest ever!

Planning Your Party
FOUR WEEKS BEFORE:
• Create your guest list. Combine guests from different occupations to provide a winning chemistry at a cocktail party or buffet. At a smaller sit-down dinner, it's best to have people who know each other at least slightly.
• Buy holiday invitations. Fill in pertinent information, address and stamp them. Mail at least three weeks ahead of time, as party dates fill up quickly during the holidays. It's perfectly alright to invite guests by telephone, but a written invitation is really best at this hectic time.
• Decide on your menu and party theme. Will you have the party catered? Will you have hired help, a bartender, or will you be handling the entire event yourself? Will it be an open house, sit-down dinner, cocktail party or brunch?
• Contact a caterer well ahead of time, if possible, to reserve the date desired. Popular catering services can be booked up to a year ahead!
• Once you have an estimate from your caterer and a firm date, you can concentrate on decorating. Do you have enough decorative holiday items? If not, what will you need to buy?
• Check for all those necessary party items, including extra ice, napkins, serving pieces, enough silver, glassware, bar items, punch bowl, cups, etc. If extras are needed, consider a party rental service.
ONE WEEK BEFORE THE PARTY:
• If you haven't already decided on your menu, check your recipe books carefully. Do not use a new recipe that will play an important part in your menu. If it should be a disaster, you would be very

disappointed. Save your new recipe experiments for less critical dishes. Important note: Don't plan a more elaborate event than you can easily handle.

• Make a list of all food items necessary. Check each recipe carefully for required ingredients.

• Buy all necessary food. Don't forget snack items such as chips, salted nuts, party mints and dips. Buy fresh items the day before the party. Buy all necessary beverages at this time, also, including alcoholic and non-alcoholic and party drink mixers.

• Make as much of the food ahead of time this week and freeze it, if possible, if you will be doing the party yourself.

• Inspect your house carefully. Freshly polished furniture and silver and gleaming crystal show guests you care about their visit to your home.

• If you will allow smoking, have ample ashtrays and matches or lighter available for your guests.

• Check your silverware and silver serving dishes. Do they need polishing? Does your good china need a washing before it is used? How about your crystal? Check your table linens and decorative holiday items for the bath.

DAY BEFORE THE PARTY:

• Complete as much of the dinner preparations as possible. You can make hors d'oeuvres, dips, wash and trim salad greens and make dessert. Many casseroles can be prepared the day before.

• Be sure you have an ample supply of ice, both for punch bowls and individual drinks.

• If you won't have time for this tomorrow, buy fresh flowers for your centerpiece, or plan a holiday arrangement that doesn't require cut flowers. If you are having a sit-down dinner, do keep the centerpiece small so conversation can flow easily. Try individual vases at each place setting.

• Be sure you have candles and that your candlesticks are available and ready to use. Have matches handy.

• If you will have a fire in your hearth during the party, be sure you lay the fire today in preparation.

• All table setting and decoration should be completed by this evening.

• You might find it helpful to compile a list of tasks you will want to do tomorrow to complete your party arrangements.

DAY OF THE PARTY:

• Plan at least an hour if possible before the party for resting and changing clothes before guests arrive.

• Finish any cooking necessary, check the table, prepare salad greens and get out all plates and serving dishes.

• Have everything you need in a handy location to serve guests mixed drinks, punch or champagne. Have all bar equipment on this table.

• Now, relax and enjoy your guests.

Secrets of a Good Holiday Party

Keep it simple. Be realistic about your capabilities and don't overextend yourself. If you're obviously exhausted, your guests won't enjoy your party, either.

If you don't like to cook or don't have time—don't! Have a few hot items catered, slice a breast of turkey, add mini rolls, an assortment of cheeses, create easy cold dips and fresh vegetable or fruit trays and you have a buffet feast that looks as if you had spent days, not hours, in the kitchen.

Remember that making people feel at home and comfortable is the one requirement of a good host. Food is always secondary, and what you serve does not have to be elaborate if there is a festive atmosphere.

Ask friends to help with easy party tasks during the evening, such as keeping dishes filled, or passing around trays of hors d'oeuvres.

Incidentally, if you have a large group of people you wish to invite but your house is small, consider the possibility of having parties on two consecutive nights. After all, you already have your house clean, silver polished, floral arrangements done and a great menu planned!

If you are having a buffet, do try to set everything up so that all guests have to carry is one plate. Rolls and butter as well as drinks and dessert will be served at individual tables.

Those Unexpected Guests

All is not lost if Cousin Samantha and her husband drop in unexpectedly with friends. Know that occasionally during this special time of year you may be caught unprepared and end up having to put things together on very short notice.

Try to keep at least one evening's worth of make-ahead snack items in your freezer, either ones you've made yourself or purchased at the supermarket. Add a loaf of cocktail rye bread, easily unthawed in a hurry in your microwave.

Keep a wedge of Brie or Camembert in the refrigerator along with a container of sour cream and packet of cream cheese. In your pantry you can store glasses of cheese spread and packets of dry dip mixes as well as pretzels, salted nuts and potato chips.

78

When guests arrive it's a simple matter of quickly putting a few of these items together and serving with a beverage.

Try placing your Brie or Camembert in an ovenproof dish, sprinkling it with chopped pistachio nuts and baking it at 350 degrees until it's soft and even a little runny. Quick and easy to serve warm as a spread on crackers, toast or fruit slices.

Add a dip mix to the sour cream, chop festive bits of red pepper and green parsley and add, and serve with fresh vegetable sticks.

Make a list of your own quick snack items for party evenings, and keep necessary ingredients on hand.

Don't Forget You!

Plan time out for beauty and relaxation during the holidays. Now is the time to have a facial, or experiment with new makeup shades, or give yourself a manicure and pedicure using holiday shades of nail polish.

Pace yourself and plan ahead. For instance, if you are having your hair cut, have it done at least two weeks before holiday parties.

On party night, ask the babysitter to arrive an hour ahead of time. Take a leisurely bath, check the house to make sure you haven't forgotten items such as fresh guest towels in the bathroom, and just rest for a few minutes before it's party time.

When the party's over, don't feel compelled to clean the kitchen immediately. There will be time in the morning, and perhaps now it would just be nice to sit in front of the fire, let the pleasant sound of soft music soothe your soul, and share your contentment after a wonderful evening with someone special.

Your Responsibilities as a Host

Although it is delightful to gather good friends together to share a wonderful evening during the holidays, as host or hostess you do have certain responsibilities to your guests.

Laws in many states now will hold you responsible if a guest who has had too much to drink at your home later causes an auto accident.

Here are some tips to help you plan a safe as well as festive celebration.

1. Don't be too quick to offer refills on drinks. It is best to allow them to finish a drink before offering another. Measure all drinks carefully, and do not provide an open bar.

2. A party doesn't mean all beverages consumed must be alcoholic. Some non-alcoholic punches are so delicious that guests may prefer them.

3. Serving food with drinks helps slow the absorption of alcohol. If guests are enjoying a delectable buffet, they are less likely to consume quantities of liquor.

4. If guests who have come in a group have a designated driver, remember to serve him or her only non-alcoholic beverages during the evening.

5. Do not serve after-dinner drinks. That is simply prolonging the effect of previous drinks and the time it will take for the alcohol to leave your guest's system.

6. At parties that the host knows may continue in to the wee hours of the morning, he or she may collect car keys when guests arrive, returning them at the end of the party only to those capable of driving.

7. For those who obviously are in no condition to drive, offer sleeping arrangements at your home, call a taxi or ask a sober friend to drive them.

13.

The Holiday Season
Red, Green—And Blue!

"I'd like to go away right now and not come back until it's over!" Carol Owens sighed.

No, this 34-year-old mother of three is not talking about the results of a flood, a death in the family or the local P.T.A. fund-raiser—but sometimes Carol feels she could cope with all three of these eventualities more easily that she does with Christmas.

"It's just gotten too overwhelming these days," the California woman confessed. "I've got too much to do. I work all week, come home and do the housework, and then on weekends I have to rush around and shop and bake and take care of creating Christmas for my kids."

"I'm just plain exhausted."

Carol isn't alone in her despair over what we normally think of as a joyous occasion. Millions of American men and women share her feelings of desperation during the holidays.

What Causes the Christmas Blues?

One therapist explains the paradox that leads to holiday depression.

"It really begins with the expectations some of us hold about the All-American family gathering. In this myth, everyone is caring toward each other, there is no anger, resentment, hostility.

"The reality, however, is often painfully at odds with this picture. This contrast between our fantasies and the truth of our own situation can be very difficult to face, and often leads to depression."

Finances Play a Part

Finances can play a potent part in creating those holiday blues.

Often the reality of our own financial picture doesn't match our expectations of being able to give relatives, our spouse, children and friends the kind of Christmas we would like them to have.

Television commercials, magazines, and peer pressure all push us toward giving gifts perhaps we really cannot afford. This is often hard to reconcile with our bank balance, and so we may go ahead and charge gifts, ignoring the debt we are accumulating in the new year.

Being Alone can be Painful at Christmas

As difficult to face as finances and the realities of our own family life are, the holiday experience can be even more devastating for those who haven't any family or who feel isolation while in the midst of their own families.

Society projects the family so much at this time of year that those without feel all the more desperate to belong.

If you live a long distance away from relatives, have recently made a move and miss old friends and haven't yet had time to make new ones, the Christmas season is a time when life is guaranteed to provide heartaches.

Ah, Those Childhood Fantasies

As children, we believed the myth of the Easter Bunny and Santa Claus. We never doubted that these fantasy figures could make our young world right.

As adults, each passing year pushes that illusion further from our grasp. We realize we must do it for ourselves, and that alone can lead to self-doubt and eventually toward depression.

We must be the grown-up now, whether we feel ready for it or not. If you are single, there is now no one to fulfill your dreams. You are on your own and it is up to you.

Married? That doesn't seem to be any easier. Your spouse may now look to you to play a part in the fulfillment of his or her fantasy holiday—which may be very different than the celebration you envision.

If you have children, their entire Christmas is in your hands. You are Santa, the Tooth Fairy, the Easter Bunny and Superwoman rolled into one.

The Dark Time of the Year

As if there weren't enough reason for feeling "down" during this time, the Christmas holidays fall during the dark time of the year, a time that traditionally should be used for self-introspection and deepening family unity.

Instead, society projects external activities such as gift giving, decorating, hosting as well as attending parties, so that the individual is left yearning for the development of deeper intimacy.

It is important to remember that during this time of the year, many strong emotions may be felt. Family problems may increase as well as feelings of alienation. You will tire more easily, perhaps find difficulty in a previously happy relationship, and generally find your stress level taking a decided turn for the worse.

However, once you realize that there may be some unusual feelings and that it is not you alone who is experiencing them, try giving yourself a week or so to just experience the emotions.

Do not tell yourself "I really shouldn't be feeling this way."

Remember, you wouldn't be this judgmental if a friend were upset.

Letting it happen, allowing ourselves to have and experience these negative feelings, may then let us turn these around into something that is positive.

Here are some tips for dealing with powerful feelings that may arise during the holidays.

When the Holidays Cause Distress:

1. Allow yourself to feel blue, but try to discover what it is about the season that is making you feel this way.

2. Recognize that the Christmas season is difficult for nearly everyone. You are not alone. Magazines, newspapers and television may depict a "reality" about this time of the year that is less than accurate.

3. Reach out to others who are lonely.

4. Become a volunteer in a helping organization.

5. Begin now adding to your support system. Invite an acquaintance to share lunch or dinner, see a play, go to a movie.

6. Become a participant in activities. Risk becoming involved. Take a class, join a club, learn to dance, take up a new sport.

7. Be honest in your expectations of a new relationship.

8. Be willing to risk sharing your feelings, and be tolerant of those who have differing ideas and goals.

9. If your depression is deepening, consult a local therapist. Even a few brief appointments may help you overcome hidden anxieties and provide support at a time when it is most needed.

10. Exercise! There is nothing like physically releasing all our tensions and cares of the day in a round of activity we enjoy, whether it's aerobics, square dancing or tennis.

11. Buy something for yourself, something you don't need but will enjoy, a gift just for you. Christmas may seem as if it's all getting things for others, but you deserve a treat, too. We all need to pamper ourselves sometimes.

12. If you're feeling down because you've been spending a lot of

energy avoiding something you know has to be done—do it! This "avoidance behavior" is a common cause of depression. Once we actually do what we've been running from, we are often surprised to find it wasn't as bad as we had anticipated. The fear was worse than the task itself.

13. Clean your apartment or move your furniture. The act of creating order out of chaos is strangely soothing.

14. Try learning something new, perhaps something you've always wanted to try but never found time for before. Yes, you're in the midst of one of the busiest seasons of the year, but take time out for you. Learning builds confidence.

And anyway, that old cliche that tells us if we want something done to ask the busiest person we know is based on fact. Somehow, the more active we are, the more we find time for.

15. Escape from it all! Consider taking your vacation during the Christmas season if you're single. A change of scene and planned holiday activities with new friends may be just what you need to rediscover the joy of the season.

If you're married, make a date with your husband. It can feel like old times when just the two of you see a play in the city and spend the night in a hotel afterward.

If this isn't possible, visit a friend, have dinner, spend the night. Expand your horizons in whatever way is possible for you.

HANDLE WITH CARE

14.

Christmas Countdown Calendar

January:

☐ 1. Buy Christmas wrapping paper, tags, ribbon, ties, gift bows and Christmas cards at winter sales, if you haven't already purchased these at December post-Christmas sales.

☐ 2. List names of those you plan to buy gifts for next Christmas.

☐ 3. Save cards from last Christmas in file folder marked with year.

☐ 4. Write thank-you notes for all gifts received at Christmas.

☐ 5. Open Christmas Club or savings account.

Other _____

_____

February:

☐ 1. Create next year's Christmas card list, using Christmas Card Record pages at back of book. Be sure to include addresses of new friends or changes of addresses of old friends in your new master card file.

☐ 2. Buy two gifts on your Christmas list, wrap, tag and put away. Shop Washington's Birthday sales.

☐ 3. Begin your Memory Box. Using a cardboard carton or large shoe box, keep clippings of articles that might interest friends, as well as other items to enclose with cards or gifts at Christmas. Label them with intended recipient's name.

Other _____

_____

March:

☐ 1. If you have an annual holiday party, take time to plan menu for this event early.

☐ 2. Decide on number of people to invite and write tentative guest list. Names can easily be added or deleted in December.

☐ 3. Buy two gifts, wrap, tag and put away.

☐ 4. Buy two boxes of thank-you notes to use during the year and after Christmas, to thank friends or relatives for gifts received, a party enjoyed, or a special favor. Stamp all envelopes. The best intentions seem to go astray when you can't find a stamp!

Other _____

_____

April:

☐ 1. Buy two gifts, wrap, tag and put away. Shop post-Easter sales.

☐ 2. Remember to complete first the purchase of all gifts which have to be mailed. Consider weight of gift as well as suitability for mailing when making purchase. Have gift wrapped for mailing at store, if possible. Pencil recipient's name lightly on reverse side.

☐ 3. Consider purchasing an inexpensive locking footlocker at a surplus supply firm in which to store your gifts until Christmas, if you have children who might be tempted to peek at packages.

Other _____

_____

May:

☐ 1. Buy two gifts, wrap, tag and put away. Memorial Day sales can be an excellent time to purchase gifts for birthdays as well as Christmas.

Other _____

_____

June:

☐ 1. Buy two gifts, wrap, tag and put away.

☐ 2. If you plan to make your Christmas cards or gifts this year, June is not too early to begin! This can be a great summer project for children during summer vacation.

Other _____

_____

July

☐ 1. Send for all mail order catalogs of interest. Keep master list of catalogs ordered, along with date requested. That will give you an indication of the firm's response time. (See Chapter Eleven, "Shopping by Mail").

☐ 2. Buy two gifts, wrap, tag and put away.

☐ 3. Continue working on gifts and/or cards you are making for the holidays.

☐ 4. Watch for "Christmas in July" sales at local stores.

Other _____

_____

August:

☐ 1. Plan three weeks of easy holiday dinners for period from December 12 until January 2.

☐ 2. Buy two gifts, wrap, tag and put away.

☐ 3. Finish making holiday gifts and cards.

☐ 4. If you are having your holiday party catered this year, call catering firm in advance, discuss your requirements, ask for estimates, and be sure the firm will be available on the date you desire. In many locales, popular caterers are booked up to a year in advance.

Other _____

_____

September:

☐ 1. Send for all items on your gift list that must be ordered from catalogs.

☐ 2. If you are not ordering by mail this year, buy two gifts, wrap and tag them and put away.

☐ 3. If you do not have a good photo of yourself or your family, plan on taking one this month while weather is still mild, if you wish to send photo greeting cards, or enclose photos with your cards.

☐ 4. Send negative to your favorite local quick-print firm for multiple copies.

Other _____

_____

October:

☐ 1. Address Christmas cards, if you haven't done so already. Write personal notes on each, if you are not enclosing a holiday letter.

☐ 2. Write Christmas letter and have it printed. Wait to buy stamps at post office until holiday stamps are in stock.

☐ 3. Buy two gifts, wrap, tag and put away.

☐ 4. If you have already set a date for your holiday party and engaged a caterer, check to make certain the date you requested has been definitely booked. Discuss the type of event you are planning, such as a holiday brunch, open house, buffet or sit-down dinner and request a preliminary estimate.

☐ 5. If you plan to do your own cooking, do consider hiring serving help to assist you. Completing all holiday entertaining plans well in advance of the season will not only allow you to secure the best help available but ensure your peace of mind during the busiest season of the year.

Other _____

_____

November:

☐ 1. Buy holiday stamps, place on all Christmas cards and letters. By the end of November, mail all cards which must travel a long distance.

☐ 2. Mail all gifts which must go out of town. Label "Do not open until Christmas" in case your gift might be mistaken for an ordinary package.

☐ 3. Buy any last-minute gifts remaining, tag and put away. Be sure you have entered all gifts purchased throughout the year on your gift planning sheet.

☐ 4. Send invitations in mid-November for your holiday party. Use menu and guest list you created in March.

☐ 5. After Thanksgiving, unpack your Christmas decorations and note anything that must be replaced or purchased to complete your decorating for the holiday season. Test light strings for burned out bulbs.

☐ 6. Shop for party snacks, including crackers, frozen hors d'oeuvres, chips and canned products, as well as cocktail items and other party serving ware necessary.

☐ 7. Make hors d'oeuvres that freeze well ahead of time. Label, date and freeze.

☐ 8. If you are planning to purchase your tree at a local Christmas tree farm, make your selection early. They will tag and keep your tree for you until you are ready to pick it up.

Other _____

_____

December:
☐ 1. RELAX! Your shopping is done! Now all you have to do is enjoy your holiday party. Now is the time to use that three-week list of easy holiday main dishes you put together earlier.

☐ 2. If you haven't done this already, prepare any Christmas food gifts that will keep well, such as nut breads, fruitcake and cookies that freeze well. Wrap and store. These are great last-minute gifts, also.

☐ 3. Do your indoor decorating. Include holiday guest towels in bathroom, and decorations in kitchen, family room and guest room.

☐ 4. Mail all Christmas cards that remain.

☐ 5. Mid-December, select your tree, if you have not already done so. Plan a special tree-decorating evening for family or friends, if desired. Store tree in bucket of water until day of decorating.

☐ 6. The day before your party, do all tasks that can be done ahead, such as decorating, table setting, setting out necessary serving dishes.

☐ 7. If desired, buy holiday tablecloth, napkins or Christmas guest towels, or wait and buy them in a few weeks at January sale events, for next Christmas.

☐ 8. Don't forget to buy extra extension cords, holiday disposable items such as napkins, coasters, plastic beverage cups and candles, extra ice cubes, bulbs to replace last-minute burn-outs, film for your camera, alcoholic and non-alcoholic beverages, fresh wreaths, greens and mistletoe, and disposable bathroom guest towels, if you have not already done so.

☐ 9. Put a few cinnamon sticks in water in a saucepan. Let simmer for 45 minutes before your party for a scent that tells guests you must have spent the day in the kitchen baking!

☐ 10. Keep a supply of small, wrapped gifts suitable for men or women. These can also substitute as hostess gifts. In addition, keep a few inexpensive extra presents suitable for children on hand.

☐ 11. Engage baby sitters early this month for any special dates you know are coming up, or arrange to trade babysitting hours with a friend.

Last—But Far From Least!

You now have time in your schedule to fulfill this season of love. Plan a visit to someone in a nursing home, help your church in its work, or assist a group preparing gifts and food for the needy.

There is an infinite variety of worthwhile activities in which you might participate. It is this involvement, this caring for others, that makes us realize anew what Christmas means.

We find out once again that it isn't about buying gifts, sending cards, decorating a tree—it's about people, and loving each other all year long, not just during the holidays. It's about helping those we can help, and offering emotional support to those who need us in other ways.

It's about sharing what we have with those we love, humming Christmas carols as we drive to work along on a crowded freeway, smelling the fresh pine scent of our holiday tree, getting a lump in the throat when our youngest proudly places a home-made decoration on the tree.

It's about how everything suddenly looks brighter, the rain isn't as wet and cold, a fire burns more vividly in the hearth, the stars shine more brightly in the winter sky.

It's stability in our changing world, the knowledge that whatever else may be different, the old customs remain the same. It's the promise of a better year next year, hope for a world that may finally welcome peace and abolish war, a world in which our children may live without fear, and we may deal with each other in trust.

If this only happens once a year, it would be a tragedy indeed were we not to "keep" Christmas in the best way possible.

If this book has helped in any way to make it possible for you to enjoy a peaceful holiday in our stressful world, it will have achieved its goal.

Merry Christmas!

RECORD OF GIFTS PURCHASED DURING YEAR

DATE	DESCRIPTION	FOR	PRICE

GIFT BUYING GUIDE

When you are planning your Christmas shopping list, take this suggested gift list along, as well as your gift profile sheet for each person for whom you plan to buy.

For:	Gift Idea:	Price Range:
Husband		
Wife		
Son		
Son		
Daughter		
Daughter		
Mother		
Father		
Grandmother		
Grandfather		
Sister(s)		
Brother(s)		
Mother-in-law		
Father-in-law		
Brother-in-law		
Sister-in-law		
Niece(s)		
Nephew(s)		
Aunt(s)		
Uncle(s)		
Employer		
Colleagues		
Postman		
Maintenance man		
Teacher(s)		
Friends		

Others _____

_____

_____

_____

_____

Gift Profile

Name _____

Age _____ Occupation_____

Hobbies _____

Other Interests _____

Favorite Colors _____

Likes: Dislikes:

Send Card and/or Gift On:		**Sizes:**

New Year's Day   _____   Dress _____

Valentine's Day   _____   Blouse _____

St. Patrick's Day   _____   Shirt _____

Passover   _____   Belt _____

Easter   _____   Slacks _____

Mother's Day   _____   Hat _____ Gloves _____

Father's Day   _____   Shoes _____

Halloween   _____

Hanukkah   _____   PRICE RANGE:

Thanksgiving   _____

Christmas   _____   _____

Birthday   _____

Anniversary   _____   _____

Dates to Remember:

Birthday _____ Anniversary _____

Spouse's Birthday _____

Children's Birthdays _____

Gift Items sent:

1986 _____   1993 _____

1987 _____   1994 _____

1988 _____   1995 _____

1989 _____   1996 _____

1990 _____   1997 _____

1991 _____   1998 _____

1992 _____   1999 _____

2000 _____

Gift Profile

Name _____

Age _____ Occupation_____

Hobbies _____

Other Interests _____

Favorite Colors _____

Likes: Dislikes:

Send Card and/or Gift On: **Sizes:**

New Year's Day   _____   Dress _____
Valentine's Day   _____   Blouse _____
St. Patrick's Day   _____   Shirt _____
Passover   _____   Belt _____
Easter   _____   Slacks _____
Mother's Day   _____   Hat _____ Gloves _____
Father's Day   _____   Shoes _____
Halloween   _____
Hanukkah   _____   PRICE RANGE:
Thanksgiving   _____
Christmas   _____   _____
Birthday   _____
Anniversary   _____   _____

Dates to Remember:

Birthday _____ Anniversary _____

Spouse's Birthday _____

Children's Birthdays _____

Gift Items sent:

1986 _____   1993 _____
1987 _____   1994 _____
1988 _____   1995 _____
1989 _____   1996 _____
1990 _____   1997 _____
1991 _____   1998 _____
1992 _____   1999 _____

2000 _____

Gift Profile

Name _____

Age _____ Occupation_____

Hobbies _____

Other Interests _____

Favorite Colors _____

Likes: Dislikes:

Send Card and/or Gift On: **Sizes:**

New Year's Day   _____   Dress _____
Valentine's Day   _____   Blouse _____
St. Patrick's Day   _____   Shirt _____
Passover   _____   Belt _____
Easter   _____   Slacks _____
Mother's Day   _____   Hat _____ Gloves _____
Father's Day   _____   Shoes _____
Halloween   _____
Hanukkah   _____   PRICE RANGE:
Thanksgiving   _____
Christmas   _____   _____
Birthday   _____
Anniversary   _____   _____

Dates to Remember:

Birthday _____ Anniversary _____

Spouse's Birthday _____

Children's Birthdays _____

Gift Items sent:

1986 _____   1993 _____
1987 _____   1994 _____
1988 _____   1995 _____
1989 _____   1996 _____
1990 _____   1997 _____
1991 _____   1998 _____
1992 _____   1999 _____
                2000 _____

Gift Profile

Name _____

Age _____ Occupation_____

Hobbies _____

Other Interests _____

Favorite Colors _____

Likes: Dislikes:

Send Card and/or Gift On: **Sizes:**

New Year's Day   _____   Dress _____

Valentine's Day   _____   Blouse _____

St. Patrick's Day   _____   Shirt _____

Passover   _____   Belt _____

Easter   _____   Slacks _____

Mother's Day   _____   Hat _____ Gloves _____

Father's Day   _____   Shoes _____

Halloween   _____

Hanukkah   _____   PRICE RANGE:

Thanksgiving   _____

Christmas   _____   _____

Birthday   _____

Anniversary   _____   _____

Dates to Remember:

Birthday _____ Anniversary _____

Spouse's Birthday _____

Children's Birthdays _____

Gift Items sent:

1986 _____   1993 _____

1987 _____   1994 _____

1988 _____   1995 _____

1989 _____   1996 _____

1990 _____   1997 _____

1991 _____   1998 _____

1992 _____   1999 _____

2000 _____

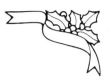

Gift Profile

Name _____

Age _____ Occupation_____

Hobbies _____

Other Interests _____

Favorite Colors _____

Likes: Dislikes:

Send Card and/or Gift On: **Sizes:**

New Year's Day   _____   Dress _____
Valentine's Day   _____   Blouse _____
St. Patrick's Day   _____   Shirt _____
Passover   _____   Belt _____
Easter   _____   Slacks _____
Mother's Day   _____   Hat _____ Gloves _____
Father's Day   _____   Shoes _____
Halloween   _____
Hanukkah   _____   PRICE RANGE:
Thanksgiving   _____
Christmas   _____   _____
Birthday   _____
Anniversary   _____   _____

Dates to Remember:

Birthday _____ Anniversary _____

Spouse's Birthday _____

Children's Birthdays _____

Gift Items sent:

1986 _____   1993 _____
1987 _____   1994 _____
1988 _____   1995 _____
1989 _____   1996 _____
1990 _____   1997 _____
1991 _____   1998 _____
1992 _____   1999 _____

2000 _____

Gift Profile

Name _____

Age _____ Occupation_____

Hobbies _____

Other Interests _____

Favorite Colors _____

Likes: Dislikes:

Send Card and/or Gift On: **Sizes:**

New Year's Day   _____   Dress _____
Valentine's Day   _____   Blouse _____
St. Patrick's Day   _____   Shirt _____
Passover   _____   Belt _____
Easter   _____   Slacks _____
Mother's Day   _____   Hat _____ Gloves _____
Father's Day   _____   Shoes _____
Halloween   _____
Hanukkah   _____   PRICE RANGE:
Thanksgiving   _____
Christmas   _____   _____
Birthday   _____
Anniversary   _____   _____

Dates to Remember:

Birthday _____ Anniversary _____

Spouse's Birthday _____

Children's Birthdays _____

Gift Items sent:

1986 _____   1993 _____
1987 _____   1994 _____
1988 _____   1995 _____
1989 _____   1996 _____
1990 _____   1997 _____
1991 _____   1998 _____
1992 _____   1999 _____

                2000 _____

Gift Profile

Name _____

Age _____ Occupation_____

Hobbies _____

Other Interests _____

Favorite Colors _____

Likes: Dislikes:

Send Card and/or Gift On: **Sizes:**

New Year's Day   _____   Dress _____

Valentine's Day   _____   Blouse _____

St. Patrick's Day   _____   Shirt _____

Passover   _____   Belt _____

Easter   _____   Slacks _____

Mother's Day   _____   Hat _____ Gloves _____

Father's Day   _____   Shoes _____

Halloween   _____

Hanukkah   _____   PRICE RANGE:

Thanksgiving   _____

Christmas   _____   _____

Birthday   _____

Anniversary   _____   _____

Dates to Remember:

Birthday _____ Anniversary _____

Spouse's Birthday _____

Children's Birthdays _____

Gift Items sent:

1986 _____   1993 _____

1987 _____   1994 _____

1988 _____   1995 _____

1989 _____   1996 _____

1990 _____   1997 _____

1991 _____   1998 _____

1992 _____   1999 _____

2000 _____

Gift Profile

Name _____

Age _____ Occupation_____

Hobbies _____

Other Interests _____

Favorite Colors _____

Likes: Dislikes:

Send Card and/or Gift On: **Sizes:**

New Year's Day   _____   Dress _____
Valentine's Day   _____   Blouse _____
St. Patrick's Day   _____   Shirt _____
Passover   _____   Belt _____
Easter   _____   Slacks _____
Mother's Day   _____   Hat _____ Gloves _____
Father's Day   _____   Shoes _____
Halloween   _____
Hanukkah   _____   PRICE RANGE:
Thanksgiving   _____
Christmas   _____   _____
Birthday   _____
Anniversary   _____   _____

Dates to Remember:

Birthday _____ Anniversary _____

Spouse's Birthday _____

Children's Birthdays _____

Gift Items sent:

1986 _____   1993 _____
1987 _____   1994 _____
1988 _____   1995 _____
1989 _____   1996 _____
1990 _____   1997 _____
1991 _____   1998 _____
1992 _____   1999 _____

        2000 _____

Gift Profile

Name _____

Age _____ Occupation_____

Hobbies _____

Other Interests _____

Favorite Colors _____

Likes: Dislikes:

Send Card and/or Gift On: **Sizes:**

New Year's Day   _____   Dress _____
Valentine's Day   _____   Blouse _____
St. Patrick's Day   _____   Shirt _____
Passover   _____   Belt _____
Easter   _____   Slacks _____
Mother's Day   _____   Hat _____ Gloves _____
Father's Day   _____   Shoes _____
Halloween   _____
Hanukkah   _____   PRICE RANGE:
Thanksgiving   _____
Christmas   _____   _____
Birthday   _____
Anniversary   _____   _____

Dates to Remember:

Birthday _____ Anniversary _____

Spouse's Birthday _____

Children's Birthdays _____

Gift Items sent:

1986 _____   1993 _____
1987 _____   1994 _____
1988 _____   1995 _____
1989 _____   1996 _____
1990 _____   1997 _____
1991 _____   1998 _____
1992 _____   1999 _____

2000 _____

Gift Profile

Name _____

Age _____ Occupation_____

Hobbies _____

Other Interests _____

Favorite Colors _____

Likes: Dislikes:

Send Card and/or Gift On: **Sizes:**

New Year's Day   _____   Dress _____

Valentine's Day   _____   Blouse _____

St. Patrick's Day   _____   Shirt _____

Passover   _____   Belt _____

Easter   _____   Slacks _____

Mother's Day   _____   Hat _____ Gloves _____

Father's Day   _____   Shoes _____

Halloween   _____

Hanukkah   _____   PRICE RANGE:

Thanksgiving   _____

Christmas   _____   _____

Birthday   _____

Anniversary   _____   _____

Dates to Remember:

Birthday _____ Anniversary _____

Spouse's Birthday _____

Children's Birthdays _____

Gift Items sent:

1986 _____   1993 _____

1987 _____   1994 _____

1988 _____   1995 _____

1989 _____   1996 _____

1990 _____   1997 _____

1991 _____   1998 _____

1992 _____   1999 _____

2000 _____

Christmas Card Record

Name _____

Address _____

Apt. or Box No. _____ Phone ( ) _____

City _____ State _____ Zip _____

Children (Names and ages) _____

Card Sent: **Card Received:**

19_____ 19_____ 19_____   19_____ 19_____ 19_____

19_____ 19_____ 19_____   19_____ 19_____ 19_____

19_____ 19_____ 19_____   19_____ 19_____ 19_____

19_____ 19_____ 20_____   19_____ 19_____ 20_____

19_____ 19_____ 20_____   19_____ 19_____ 20_____

****

Name _____

Address _____

Apt. or Box No. _____ Phone ( ) _____

City _____ State _____ Zip _____

Children (Names and ages) _____

Card Sent: **Card Received:**

19_____ 19_____ 19_____   19_____ 19_____ 19_____

19_____ 19_____ 19_____   19_____ 19_____ 19_____

19_____ 19_____ 19_____   19_____ 19_____ 19_____

19_____ 19_____ 20_____   19_____ 19_____ 20_____

19_____ 19_____ 20_____   19_____ 19_____ 20_____

****

Name _____

Address _____

Apt. or Box No. _____ Phone ( ) _____

City _____ State _____ Zip _____

Children (Names and ages) _____

Card Sent: **Card Received:**

19_____ 19_____ 19_____   19_____ 19_____ 19_____

19_____ 19_____ 19_____   19_____ 19_____ 19_____

19_____ 19_____ 19_____   19_____ 19_____ 19_____

19_____ 19_____ 20_____   19_____ 19_____ 20_____

19_____ 19_____ 20_____   19_____ 19_____ 20_____

Christmas Card Record

Name _____
Address _____
Apt. or Box No. _____ Phone ( ) _____
City _____ State _____ Zip _____
Children (Names and ages) _____
_____

Card Sent:			**Card Received:**		
19_____	19_____	19_____	19_____	19_____	19_____
19_____	19_____	19_____	19_____	19_____	19_____
19_____	19_____	19_____	19_____	19_____	19_____
19_____	19_____	20_____	19_____	19_____	20_____
19_____	19_____	20_____	19_____	19_____	20_____

****

Name _____
Address _____
Apt. or Box No. _____ Phone ( ) _____
City _____ State _____ Zip _____
Children (Names and ages) _____
_____

Card Sent:			**Card Received:**		
19_____	19_____	19_____	19_____	19_____	19_____
19_____	19_____	19_____	19_____	19_____	19_____
19_____	19_____	19_____	19_____	19_____	19_____
19_____	19_____	20_____	19_____	19_____	20_____
19_____	19_____	20_____	19_____	19_____	20_____

****

Name _____
Address _____
Apt. or Box No. _____ Phone ( ) _____
City _____ State _____ Zip _____
Children (Names and ages) _____
_____

Card Sent:			**Card Received:**		
19_____	19_____	19_____	19_____	19_____	19_____
19_____	19_____	19_____	19_____	19_____	19_____
19_____	19_____	19_____	19_____	19_____	19_____
19_____	19_____	20_____	19_____	19_____	20_____
19_____	19_____	20_____	19_____	19_____	20_____

Christmas Card Record

Name _____

Address _____

Apt. or Box No. _____ Phone ( ) _____

City _____ State _____ Zip _____

Children (Names and ages) _____

_____

Card Sent: **Card Received:**

19____ 19____ 19____   19____ 19____ 19____

19____ 19____ 19____   19____ 19____ 19____

19____ 19____ 19____   19____ 19____ 19____

19____ 19____ 20____   19____ 19____ 20____

19____ 19____ 20____   19____ 19____ 20____

****

Name _____

Address _____

Apt. or Box No. _____ Phone ( ) _____

City _____ State _____ Zip _____

Children (Names and ages) _____

_____

Card Sent: **Card Received:**

19____ 19____ 19____   19____ 19____ 19____

19____ 19____ 19____   19____ 19____ 19____

19____ 19____ 19____   19____ 19____ 19____

19____ 19____ 20____   19____ 19____ 20____

19____ 19____ 20____   19____ 19____ 20____

****

Name _____

Address _____

Apt. or Box No. _____ Phone ( ) _____

City _____ State _____ Zip _____

Children (Names and ages) _____

_____

Card Sent: **Card Received:**

19____ 19____ 19____   19____ 19____ 19____

19____ 19____ 19____   19____ 19____ 19____

19____ 19____ 19____   19____ 19____ 19____

19____ 19____ 20____   19____ 19____ 20____

19____ 19____ 20____   19____ 19____ 20____

Christmas Card Record

Name _____
Address _____
Apt. or Box No. _____ Phone ( ) _____
City _____ State _____ Zip _____
Children (Names and ages) _____

_____

Card Sent: **Card Received:**

19____ 19____ 19____   19____ 19____ 19____
19____ 19____ 19____   19____ 19____ 19____
19____ 19____ 19____   19____ 19____ 19____
19____ 19____ 20____   19____ 19____ 20____
19____ 19____ 20____   19____ 19____ 20____

****

Name _____
Address _____
Apt. or Box No. _____ Phone ( ) _____
City _____ State _____ Zip _____
Children (Names and ages) _____

_____

Card Sent: **Card Received:**

19____ 19____ 19____   19____ 19____ 19____
19____ 19____ 19____   19____ 19____ 19____
19____ 19____ 19____   19____ 19____ 19____
19____ 19____ 20____   19____ 19____ 20____
19____ 19____ 20____   19____ 19____ 20____

****

Name _____
Address _____
Apt. or Box No. _____ Phone ( ) _____
City _____ State _____ Zip _____
Children (Names and ages) _____

_____

Card Sent: **Card Received:**

19____ 19____ 19____   19____ 19____ 19____
19____ 19____ 19____   19____ 19____ 19____
19____ 19____ 19____   19____ 19____ 19____
19____ 19____ 20____   19____ 19____ 20____
19____ 19____ 20____   19____ 19____ 20____

Christmas Card Record

Name _____
Address _____
Apt. or Box No. _____ Phone (____) _____
City _____ State _____ Zip _____
Children (Names and ages) _____
_____

Card Sent:			**Card Received:**		
19____	19____	19____	19____	19____	19____
19____	19____	19____	19____	19____	19____
19____	19____	19____	19____	19____	19____
19____	19____	20____	19____	19____	20____
19____	19____	20____	19____	19____	20____

****

Name _____
Address _____
Apt. or Box No. _____ Phone (____) _____
City _____ State _____ Zip _____
Children (Names and ages) _____
_____

Card Sent:			**Card Received:**		
19____	19____	19____	19____	19____	19____
19____	19____	19____	19____	19____	19____
19____	19____	19____	19____	19____	19____
19____	19____	20____	19____	19____	20____
19____	19____	20____	19____	19____	20____

****

Name _____
Address _____
Apt. or Box No. _____ Phone (____) _____
City _____ State _____ Zip _____
Children (Names and ages) _____
_____

Card Sent:			**Card Received:**		
19____	19____	19____	19____	19____	19____
19____	19____	19____	19____	19____	19____
19____	19____	19____	19____	19____	19____
19____	19____	20____	19____	19____	20____
19____	19____	20____	19____	19____	20____

Christmas Card Record

Name _____

Address _____

Apt. or Box No. _____ Phone ( ) _____

City _____ State _____ Zip _____

Children (Names and ages) _____

_____

Card Sent: **Card Received:**

19_____ 19_____ 19_____   19_____ 19_____ 19_____

19_____ 19_____ 19_____   19_____ 19_____ 19_____

19_____ 19_____ 19_____   19_____ 19_____ 19_____

19_____ 19_____ 20_____   19_____ 19_____ 20_____

19_____ 19_____ 20_____   19_____ 19_____ 20_____

****

Name _____

Address _____

Apt. or Box No. _____ Phone ( ) _____

City _____ State _____ Zip _____

Children (Names and ages) _____

_____

Card Sent: **Card Received:**

19_____ 19_____ 19_____   19_____ 19_____ 19_____

19_____ 19_____ 19_____   19_____ 19_____ 19_____

19_____ 19_____ 19_____   19_____ 19_____ 19_____

19_____ 19_____ 20_____   19_____ 19_____ 20_____

19_____ 19_____ 20_____   19_____ 19_____ 20_____

****

Name _____

Address _____

Apt. or Box No. _____ Phone ( ) _____

City _____ State _____ Zip _____

Children (Names and ages) _____

_____

Card Sent: **Card Received:**

19_____ 19_____ 19_____   19_____ 19_____ 19_____

19_____ 19_____ 19_____   19_____ 19_____ 19_____

19_____ 19_____ 19_____   19_____ 19_____ 19_____

19_____ 19_____ 20_____   19_____ 19_____ 20_____

19_____ 19_____ 20_____   19_____ 19_____ 20_____

Christmas Card Record

Name _____
Address _____
Apt. or Box No. _____ Phone ( ) _____
City _____ State _____ Zip _____
Children (Names and ages) _____
_____

Card Sent: **Card Received:**
19_____ 19_____ 19_____   19_____ 19_____ 19_____
19_____ 19_____ 19_____   19_____ 19_____ 19_____
19_____ 19_____ 19_____   19_____ 19_____ 19_____
19_____ 19_____ 20_____   19_____ 19_____ 20_____
19_____ 19_____ 20_____   19_____ 19_____ 20_____

****

Name _____
Address _____
Apt. or Box No. _____ Phone ( ) _____
City _____ State _____ Zip _____
Children (Names and ages) _____
_____

Card Sent: **Card Received:**
19_____ 19_____ 19_____   19_____ 19_____ 19_____
19_____ 19_____ 19_____   19_____ 19_____ 19_____
19_____ 19_____ 19_____   19_____ 19_____ 19_____
19_____ 19_____ 20_____   19_____ 19_____ 20_____
19_____ 19_____ 20_____   19_____ 19_____ 20_____

****

Name _____
Address _____
Apt. or Box No. _____ Phone ( ) _____
City _____ State _____ Zip _____
Children (Names and ages) _____
_____

Card Sent: **Card Received:**
19_____ 19_____ 19_____   19_____ 19_____ 19_____
19_____ 19_____ 19_____   19_____ 19_____ 19_____
19_____ 19_____ 19_____   19_____ 19_____ 19_____
19_____ 19_____ 20_____   19_____ 19_____ 20_____
19_____ 19_____ 20_____   19_____ 19_____ 20_____

Christmas Card Record

Name _____

Address _____

Apt. or Box No. _____ Phone ( ) _____

City _____ State _____ Zip _____

Children (Names and ages) _____

_____

Card Sent: **Card Received:**

19_____ 19_____ 19_____   19_____ 19_____ 19_____

19_____ 19_____ 19_____   19_____ 19_____ 19_____

19_____ 19_____ 19_____   19_____ 19_____ 19_____

19_____ 19_____ 20_____   19_____ 19_____ 20_____

19_____ 19_____ 20_____   19_____ 19_____ 20_____

****

Name _____

Address _____

Apt. or Box No. _____ Phone ( ) _____

City _____ State _____ Zip _____

Children (Names and ages) _____

_____

Card Sent: **Card Received:**

19_____ 19_____ 19_____   19_____ 19_____ 19_____

19_____ 19_____ 19_____   19_____ 19_____ 19_____

19_____ 19_____ 19_____   19_____ 19_____ 19_____

19_____ 19_____ 20_____   19_____ 19_____ 20_____

19_____ 19_____ 20_____   19_____ 19_____ 20_____

****

Name _____

Address _____

Apt. or Box No. _____ Phone ( ) _____

City _____ State _____ Zip _____

Children (Names and ages) _____

_____

Card Sent: **Card Received:**

19_____ 19_____ 19_____   19_____ 19_____ 19_____

19_____ 19_____ 19_____   19_____ 19_____ 19_____

19_____ 19_____ 19_____   19_____ 19_____ 19_____

19_____ 19_____ 20_____   19_____ 19_____ 20_____

19_____ 19_____ 20_____   19_____ 19_____ 20_____

Christmas Card Record

Name _____

Address _____

Apt. or Box No. _____ Phone ( ) _____

City _____ State _____ Zip _____

Children (Names and ages) _____

Card Sent:			**Card Received:**		
19_____	19_____	19_____	19_____	19_____	19_____
19_____	19_____	19_____	19_____	19_____	19_____
19_____	19_____	19_____	19_____	19_____	19_____
19_____	19_____	20_____	19_____	19_____	20_____
19_____	19_____	20_____	19_____	19_____	20_____

****

Name _____

Address _____

Apt. or Box No. _____ Phone ( ) _____

City _____ State _____ Zip _____

Children (Names and ages) _____

Card Sent:			**Card Received:**		
19_____	19_____	19_____	19_____	19_____	19_____
19_____	19_____	19_____	19_____	19_____	19_____
19_____	19_____	19_____	19_____	19_____	19_____
19_____	19_____	20_____	19_____	19_____	20_____
19_____	19_____	20_____	19_____	19_____	20_____

****

Name _____

Address _____

Apt. or Box No. _____ Phone ( ) _____

City _____ State _____ Zip _____

Children (Names and ages) _____

Card Sent:			**Card Received:**		
19_____	19_____	19_____	19_____	19_____	19_____
19_____	19_____	19_____	19_____	19_____	19_____
19_____	19_____	19_____	19_____	19_____	19_____
19_____	19_____	20_____	19_____	19_____	20_____
19_____	19_____	20_____	19_____	19_____	20_____

Christmas Card Record

Name _____

Address _____

Apt. or Box No. _____ Phone ( ) _____

City _____ State _____ Zip _____

Children (Names and ages) _____

_____

Card Sent:			**Card Received:**		
19_____	19_____	19_____	19_____	19_____	19_____
19_____	19_____	19_____	19_____	19_____	19_____
19_____	19_____	19_____	19_____	19_____	19_____
19_____	19_____	20_____	19_____	19_____	20_____
19_____	19_____	20_____	19_____	19_____	20_____

****

Name _____

Address _____

Apt. or Box No. _____ Phone ( ) _____

City _____ State _____ Zip _____

Children (Names and ages) _____

_____

Card Sent:			**Card Received:**		
19_____	19_____	19_____	19_____	19_____	19_____
19_____	19_____	19_____	19_____	19_____	19_____
19_____	19_____	19_____	19_____	19_____	19_____
19_____	19_____	20_____	19_____	19_____	20_____
19_____	19_____	20_____	19_____	19_____	20_____

****

Name _____

Address _____

Apt. or Box No. _____ Phone ( ) _____

City _____ State _____ Zip _____

Children (Names and ages) _____

_____

Card Sent:			**Card Received:**		
19_____	19_____	19_____	19_____	19_____	19_____
19_____	19_____	19_____	19_____	19_____	19_____
19_____	19_____	19_____	19_____	19_____	19_____
19_____	19_____	20_____	19_____	19_____	20_____
19_____	19_____	20_____	19_____	19_____	20_____

Christmas Card Record

Name _____
Address _____
Apt. or Box No. _____ Phone ( ) _____
City _____ State _____ Zip _____
Children (Names and ages) _____

Card Sent:

19____	19____	19____
19____	19____	19____
19____	19____	19____
19____	19____	20____
19____	19____	20____

Card Received:

19____	19____	19____
19____	19____	19____
19____	19____	19____
19____	19____	20____
19____	19____	20____

****

Name _____
Address _____
Apt. or Box No. _____ Phone ( ) _____
City _____ State _____ Zip _____
Children (Names and ages) _____

Card Sent:

19____	19____	19____
19____	19____	19____
19____	19____	19____
19____	19____	20____
19____	19____	20____

Card Received:

19____	19____	19____
19____	19____	19____
19____	19____	19____
19____	19____	20____
19____	19____	20____

****

Name _____
Address _____
Apt. or Box No. _____ Phone ( ) _____
City _____ State _____ Zip _____
Children (Names and ages) _____

Card Sent:

19____	19____	19____
19____	19____	19____
19____	19____	19____
19____	19____	20____
19____	19____	20____

Card Received:

19____	19____	19____
19____	19____	19____
19____	19____	19____
19____	19____	20____
19____	19____	20____

Christmas Card Record

Name _____
Address _____
Apt. or Box No. _____ Phone ( ) _____
City _____ State _____ Zip _____
Children (Names and ages) _____
_____

Card Sent: **Card Received:**
19_____ 19_____ 19_____   19_____ 19_____ 19_____
19_____ 19_____ 19_____   19_____ 19_____ 19_____
19_____ 19_____ 19_____   19_____ 19_____ 19_____
19_____ 19_____ 20_____   19_____ 19_____ 20_____
19_____ 19_____ 20_____   19_____ 19_____ 20_____
****

Name _____
Address _____
Apt. or Box No. _____ Phone ( ) _____
City _____ State _____ Zip _____
Children (Names and ages) _____
_____

Card Sent: **Card Received:**
19_____ 19_____ 19_____   19_____ 19_____ 19_____
19_____ 19_____ 19_____   19_____ 19_____ 19_____
19_____ 19_____ 19_____   19_____ 19_____ 19_____
19_____ 19_____ 20_____   19_____ 19_____ 20_____
19_____ 19_____ 20_____   19_____ 19_____ 20_____
****

Name _____
Address _____
Apt. or Box No. _____ Phone ( ) _____
City _____ State _____ Zip _____
Children (Names and ages) _____
_____

Card Sent: **Card Received:**
19_____ 19_____ 19_____   19_____ 19_____ 19_____
19_____ 19_____ 19_____   19_____ 19_____ 19_____
19_____ 19_____ 19_____   19_____ 19_____ 19_____
19_____ 19_____ 20_____   19_____ 19_____ 20_____
19_____ 19_____ 20_____   19_____ 19_____ 20_____

Christmas Card Record

Name _____
Address _____
Apt. or Box No. _____ Phone (___) _____
City _____ State _____ Zip _____
Children (Names and ages) _____
_____

Card Sent: **Card Received:**

19____	19____	19____	19____	19____	19____
19____	19____	19____	19____	19____	19____
19____	19____	19____	19____	19____	19____
19____	19____	20____	19____	19____	20____
19____	19____	20____	19____	19____	20____

****

Name _____
Address _____
Apt. or Box No. _____ Phone (___) _____
City _____ State _____ Zip _____
Children (Names and ages) _____
_____

Card Sent: **Card Received:**

19____	19____	19____	19____	19____	19____
19____	19____	19____	19____	19____	19____
19____	19____	19____	19____	19____	19____
19____	19____	20____	19____	19____	20____
19____	19____	20____	19____	19____	20____

****

Name _____
Address _____
Apt. or Box No. _____ Phone (___) _____
City _____ State _____ Zip _____
Children (Names and ages) _____
_____

Card Sent: **Card Received:**

19____	19____	19____	19____	19____	19____
19____	19____	19____	19____	19____	19____
19____	19____	19____	19____	19____	19____
19____	19____	20____	19____	19____	20____
19____	19____	20____	19____	19____	20____

Christmas Card Record

Name _____

Address _____

Apt. or Box No. _____ Phone ( ) _____

City _____ State _____ Zip _____

Children (Names and ages) _____

_____

Card Sent: **Card Received:**

19____   19____   19____   19____   19____   19____

19____   19____   19____   19____   19____   19____

19____   19____   19____   19____   19____   19____

19____   19____   20____   19____   19____   20____

19____   19____   20____   19____   19____   20____

****

Name _____

Address _____

Apt. or Box No. _____ Phone ( ) _____

City _____ State _____ Zip _____

Children (Names and ages) _____

_____

Card Sent: **Card Received:**

19____   19____   19____   19____   19____   19____

19____   19____   19____   19____   19____   19____

19____   19____   19____   19____   19____   19____

19____   19____   20____   19____   19____   20____

19____   19____   20____   19____   19____   20____

****

Name _____

Address _____

Apt. or Box No. _____ Phone ( ) _____

City _____ State _____ Zip _____

Children (Names and ages) _____

_____

Card Sent: **Card Received:**

19____   19____   19____   19____   19____   19____

19____   19____   19____   19____   19____   19____

19____   19____   19____   19____   19____   19____

19____   19____   20____   19____   19____   20____

19____   19____   20____   19____   19____   20____

Christmas Card Record

Name _____
Address _____
Apt. or Box No. _____ Phone (   ) _____
City _____ State _____ Zip _____
Children (Names and ages) _____
_____

Card Sent: **Card Received:**

19____ 19____ 19____   19____ 19____ 19____
19____ 19____ 19____   19____ 19____ 19____
19____ 19____ 19____   19____ 19____ 19____
19____ 19____ 20____   19____ 19____ 20____
19____ 19____ 20____   19____ 19____ 20____

****

Name _____
Address _____
Apt. or Box No. _____ Phone (   ) _____
City _____ State _____ Zip _____
Children (Names and ages) _____
_____

Card Sent: **Card Received:**

19____ 19____ 19____   19____ 19____ 19____
19____ 19____ 19____   19____ 19____ 19____
19____ 19____ 19____   19____ 19____ 19____
19____ 19____ 20____   19____ 19____ 20____
19____ 19____ 20____   19____ 19____ 20____

****

Name _____
Address _____
Apt. or Box No. _____ Phone (   ) _____
City _____ State _____ Zip _____
Children (Names and ages) _____
_____

Card Sent: **Card Received:**

19____ 19____ 19____   19____ 19____ 19____
19____ 19____ 19____   19____ 19____ 19____
19____ 19____ 19____   19____ 19____ 19____
19____ 19____ 20____   19____ 19____ 20____
19____ 19____ 20____   19____ 19____ 20____

Christmas Card Record

Name _____
Address _____
Apt. or Box No. _____ Phone ( ) _____
City _____ State _____ Zip _____
Children (Names and ages) _____
_____

Card Sent: **Card Received:**

19_____   19_____   19_____   19_____   19_____   19_____
19_____   19_____   19_____   19_____   19_____   19_____
19_____   19_____   19_____   19_____   19_____   19_____
19_____   19_____   20_____   19_____   19_____   20_____
19_____   19_____   20_____   19_____   19_____   20_____

****

Name _____
Address _____
Apt. or Box No. _____ Phone ( ) _____
City _____ State _____ Zip _____
Children (Names and ages) _____
_____

Card Sent: **Card Received:**

19_____   19_____   19_____   19_____   19_____   19_____
19_____   19_____   19_____   19_____   19_____   19_____
19_____   19_____   19_____   19_____   19_____   19_____
19_____   19_____   20_____   19_____   19_____   20_____
19_____   19_____   20_____   19_____   19_____   20_____

****

Name _____
Address _____
Apt. or Box No. _____ Phone ( ) _____
City _____ State _____ Zip _____
Children (Names and ages) _____
_____

Card Sent: **Card Received:**

19_____   19_____   19_____   19_____   19_____   19_____
19_____   19_____   19_____   19_____   19_____   19_____
19_____   19_____   19_____   19_____   19_____   19_____
19_____   19_____   20_____   19_____   19_____   20_____
19_____   19_____   20_____   19_____   19_____   20_____

Christmas Card Record

Name _____

Address _____

Apt. or Box No. _____ Phone ( ) _____

City _____ State _____ Zip _____

Children (Names and ages) _____

_____

Card Sent: **Card Received:**

19_____ 19_____ 19_____   19_____ 19_____ 19_____

19_____ 19_____ 19_____   19_____ 19_____ 19_____

19_____ 19_____ 19_____   19_____ 19_____ 19_____

19_____ 19_____ 20_____   19_____ 19_____ 20_____

19_____ 19_____ 20_____   19_____ 19_____ 20_____

****

Name _____

Address _____

Apt. or Box No. _____ Phone ( ) _____

City _____ State _____ Zip _____

Children (Names and ages) _____

_____

Card Sent: **Card Received:**

19_____ 19_____ 19_____   19_____ 19_____ 19_____

19_____ 19_____ 19_____   19_____ 19_____ 19_____

19_____ 19_____ 19_____   19_____ 19_____ 19_____

19_____ 19_____ 20_____   19_____ 19_____ 20_____

19_____ 19_____ 20_____   19_____ 19_____ 20_____

****

Name _____

Address _____

Apt. or Box No. _____ Phone ( ) _____

City _____ State _____ Zip _____

Children (Names and ages) _____

_____

Card Sent: **Card Received:**

19_____ 19_____ 19_____   19_____ 19_____ 19_____

19_____ 19_____ 19_____   19_____ 19_____ 19_____

19_____ 19_____ 19_____   19_____ 19_____ 19_____

19_____ 19_____ 20_____   19_____ 19_____ 20_____

19_____ 19_____ 20_____   19_____ 19_____ 20_____

Christmas Card Record

Name _____
Address _____
Apt. or Box No. _____ Phone ( ) _____
City _____ State _____ Zip _____
Children (Names and ages) _____
_____

Card Sent: **Card Received:**

19_____   19_____   19_____   19_____   19_____   19_____
19_____   19_____   19_____   19_____   19_____   19_____
19_____   19_____   19_____   19_____   19_____   19_____
19_____   19_____   20_____   19_____   19_____   20_____
19_____   19_____   20_____   19_____   19_____   20_____

****

Name _____
Address _____
Apt. or Box No. _____ Phone ( ) _____
City _____ State _____ Zip _____
Children (Names and ages) _____
_____

Card Sent: **Card Received:**

19_____   19_____   19_____   19_____   19_____   19_____
19_____   19_____   19_____   19_____   19_____   19_____
19_____   19_____   19_____   19_____   19_____   19_____
19_____   19_____   20_____   19_____   19_____   20_____
19_____   19_____   20_____   19_____   19_____   20_____

****

Name _____
Address _____
Apt. or Box No. _____ Phone ( ) _____
City _____ State _____ Zip _____
Children (Names and ages) _____
_____

Card Sent: **Card Received:**

19_____   19_____   19_____   19_____   19_____   19_____
19_____   19_____   19_____   19_____   19_____   19_____
19_____   19_____   19_____   19_____   19_____   19_____
19_____   19_____   20_____   19_____   19_____   20_____
19_____   19_____   20_____   19_____   19_____   20_____

Order Form

H O U R   P R E S S
P.O. Box 12743, Northgate Station
San Rafael, CA 94913-2743

Please send me _____ copies of "Holiday Handbook," at $8.95 each. I understand that I may return books for a full refund if not satisfied. Please mail book order to:

Name: _____
        (Please Print)

Address: _____
          Street   Apt. #

_____
State   Zip Code

CALIFORNIANS: Please add 54 cents sales tax for each copy ordered.

SHIPPING: $1 for the first book, and 25 cents for each additional book.

Order Form

H O U R   P R E S S
P.O. Box 12743, Northgate Station
San Rafael, CA 94913-2743

Please send me _____ copies of "Holiday Handbook," at $8.95 each. I understand that I may return books for a full refund if not satisfied. Please mail book order to:

Name: _____
        (Please Print)

Address: _____
          Street   Apt. #

_____
State   Zip Code

CALIFORNIANS: Please add 54 cents sales tax for each copy ordered.

SHIPPING: $1 for the first book, and 25 cents for each additional book.